# The End of a University
From *Bildung* and *ruins* to *nonsense*

# Complicated

## A Book Series of Curriculum Studies

William F. Pinar
*Series Editor*

Volume 65

Vladimer Luarsabishvili and Maia Kiladze

# The End of a University
From *Bildung* and *ruins* to *nonsense*

PETER LANG
New York · Berlin · Bruxelles · Chennai · Lausanne · Oxford

Library of Congress Cataloging-in-Publication Data

Names: Luarsabishvili, Vladimer, 1978- author. | Kiladze, Maia, 1977- author.
Title: The end of a university : from Bildung and ruins to nonsense /
  Vladimer Luarsabishvili, Maia Kiladze.
Description: New York : Peter Lang, [2025] | Series: Complicated
  conversation, 1534-2816 ; vol. 65 | Includes bibliographical references
  and index.
Identifiers: LCCN 2025002188 (print) | LCCN 2025002189 (ebook) | ISBN
  9783034355506 (paperback) | ISBN 9783034357289 (pdf) | ISBN
  9783034357296 (epub)
Subjects: LCSH: Education, Higher—Aims and objectives. | Educational
  change. | Universities and colleges.
Classification: LCC LB2322.2 .L837 2025 (print) | LCC LB2322.2 (ebook) |
  DDC 378—dc23/eng/20250225
LC record available at https://lccn.loc.gov/2025002188
LC ebook record available at https://lccn.loc.gov/2025002189

Bibliographic Information published by the Deutsche Nationalbibliothek
The Deutsche Nationalbibliothek lists this publication in the Deutsche
Nationalbibliografie; detailed bibliographic data is available
online at http://dnb.d-nb.de.

Cover design by Peter Lang Group AG
Cover image courtesy of Vladimer Luarsabishvili

ISSN 1534-2816
ISBN 978-3-0343-5550-6 (Print)
E-ISBN 978-3-0343-5728-9 (E-PDF)
E-ISBN 978-3-0343-5729-6 (E-PUB)
DOI 10.3726/b22728

© 2025 Peter Lang Group AG, Lausanne (Switzerland)
Published by Peter Lang Publishing Inc., New York, USA
info@peterlang.com - www.peterlang.com

All rights reserved.
All parts of this publication are protected by copyright.
Any utilization outside the strict limits of the copyright law, without the permission of the publisher, is forbidden and liable to prosecution.
This applies in particular to reproductions, translations, microfilming, and storage and processing in electronic retrieval systems.

This publication has been peer reviewed.

*To Maia and Ana*

# CONTENTS

|  |  |  |
|---|---|---|
|  | Preface | 9 |
|  | Introduction | 15 |
| Chapter 1. | Historical Background | 29 |
| Chapter 2. | Education | 53 |
| Chapter 3. | Research | 71 |
| Chapter 4. | Modern University | 85 |
| Chapter 5. | Case Study: Teaching and Research in Georgia | 105 |
| Chapter 6. | Human Happiness | 119 |
| Chapter 7. | Conclusions | 129 |
|  | Postscript | 135 |
|  | Index | 145 |

# Preface

The content for a book of essays on education and research at the modern university may be composed using different approaches. The first and most frequent approach should be an attempt to cover the basic ways of organizing education as a process and as a product in and for the contemporary world. From this perspective, the task seems quite diverse and complex. On the one hand, different cultures have different expectations for educational policies, and on the other hand, the traditions of organizing educational systems also differ. Naturally, expectations arise from traditions, but the lack of certain traditions may easily result in unrealized expectations. Today, the demand for modern education, which may be different from traditional education, is high. Students from developing countries move to more developed ones to receive education, and sometimes to simply purchase a diploma. The latter is especially evident and frequently observable in some developing countries that offer easy ways to graduate. In this case, education is converted into a business, losing its professional and ethical dimensions, and is characterized by low-quality, ill-structured programs, and the absence of evidence-based research at all levels of university studies (bachelor's, master's, PhD). Marketization of higher education is observable.[1]

Another approach to composing content can be the description and analysis of modern technical possibilities that find a way into both teaching and research. E-learning, as well as access to different scientific databases, provide novel and quite attractive instruments for students, possibilities that can be beneficial from economical and communicational perspectives. Simultaneously, the rapid dissemination of new research data will in turn deepen learning that can be pursued without additional physical and financial difficulties. This approach to the content would be not only modern but also diverse and informative, drawing a distinction between the "pursuit of learning" and the "acquisition of information."[2]

Equally interesting could be the evaluation of the role of the ethical component in teaching and research, which can also form an axis for the content of the present book. Ethics from different perspectives: ethics in teaching (why, what, and how we teach), ethics in research (scientific misconduct), and ethics as an instrument for the formation of modern citizens (civic responsibility).

All three approaches make it possible to imagine a book of essays on university education and research that has a broad scope and is not limited to scholastic and traditional understanding of the topic. Additionally, critical moments experienced by human society may also be discussed, such as epidemics and pandemics,[3] giving space to reflect on the organization of medical services and respect for basic human rights during humanitarian catastrophes.

The basis of all the mentioned approaches is the three-dimensional understanding of a scientific idea, according to which a) science and opinion are indistinguishable, b) science is understood as an institution (including pedagogical and research perspectives), and c) science is a form of life.[4] Accepting all three characteristics and placing them at the center of the discussion makes understandable the role of education and research in the development of modern societies.

Keeping in mind all the aforementioned, we have decided to use all three approaches for our book. In it, we shall discuss different traditions of organizing educational systems; briefly overview the role and innovative methods of prominent philosophers of education, whose ideas strongly determined the development of the field in the nineteenth and twentieth centuries and continue to have an important impact on it today. Naturally, there are countries with more developed educational traditions, and there are others where education was not always at the forefront of social life. At the same time, many countries today offer educational services that form the international educational market and frequently determine the formation of new perceptions of educational policies. All these will be discussed from the practical, professional perspectives of the authors of this book, who collectively have more than twenty years of active teaching and research experience.

We shall also write about the role of technical development in education. From this point of view, the syntagmatic expression "philosophy of education" acquires another, probably novel, meaning. Here "philosophy" means modern ways of understanding the nature of education, linking it with market expectations. How technical progress can facilitate and sometimes ease education, both as a process and as a product, will be discussed here. It will be discovered that from educational perspectives, technical progress may be not only positive but also quite negative, leading to the formation of some perverse educational behavior, such as intentionally missing lectures by lecturers and almost totalitarian control of lecturers by university administration. The lack of mutual trust and respect between academic and administrative staff will deteriorate teaching and leave no room for university research, transforming the latter into a sham and a grand illusion.

We also dedicate a special section to the role of public health in university research. Being a special dimension that unites social and biomedical sciences and informs the health arena, public health offers contemporary insights for planning and implementing research procedures and analyzing research data. As Jürgen Mittelstrass has noted, "certain problems cannot be captured by a single discipline," especially in cases of environment, energy, and health.[5] If we aim to discover the place and role of modern education and research possibilities in the framework of the future well-being of human society, a public health research perspective could be a useful dimension for understanding the role of modern universities in our lives. Hence our interest in discussing its possibilities for building a healthy and informed society.

All the analysis offered in the book is not of a mere theoretical character. Rather, we consider this book to be a kind of case study, as in Chapter 5 we discuss the teaching and research peculiarities observed by us in Georgian universities. Our main intention for writing and including this chapter was to offer a case study of the concrete difficulties that Georgian universities face today and that may be, more or less, observable at other universities in distinct parts of the world.

Chapter 6 describes the notion of *human happiness* from historical perspective; it also tries to find the role of happiness in the building and managing of modern universities, along with the achieving the main goal of social self-realization.

All the analyzed difficulties will lead to the ethical corruption of modern universities; nobody should be responsible for anything, and teaching will be transformed from a highly ethical act into a mere financial and business operation. Lack of respect and understanding of the basic challenges in the framework of modern educational systems will lead to the loss of the key idea regarding education—opening doors for multiple individual possibilities and the formation of the responsible citizen. As Bill Readings noted, "Such is the situation of the posthistorical University, the University without an idea"[6]—and we are very much afraid that modern universities may continue their way from *Bildung*[7] and *ruins*[8] to *nonsense*.[9]

*Vladimer Luarsabishvili, Maia Kiladze*
*Tbilisi, February 27, 2024*

## Notes

1. Gibbs, 2002, 2011, 2017, 2020; Molesworth et al., 2009; Hemsley-Brown, 2011.
2. Fuller (ed.), 1989.
3. Among the books on the COVID-19 pandemic, see Osterholm and Olshaker, 2020; MacKenzie, 2020; León, 2020; Loewe, 2020; Steiner and Veel, 2021; Feierstein, 2021; Rallo Gruss (ed.) 2022; Crepaz et al., 2022; Chari and Rozas, 2022; Gallego Cuiñas, Pérez Tapias (eds.), 2022; Cooper et al., 2023; Bernhagen and Kybelka, 2024; Kiladze and Luarsabishvili, 2024.
4. Mittelstrass, 2018, p. 148.
5. Ibid., p. 58.
6. Readings, 1999, p. 118.
7. On *Bildung*, see Bollenbeck, 1994; Geuss, 1996; Masschelein and Ricken, 2003; Wimmer, 2013; Schmidt, 2013.
8. On *ruins*, see LaCapra, 1998; Readings, 1999.
9. On the *end of universities*, see Tehranian, 1996; Pan, 1998.

## Bibliography

Bernhagen, P. and Kybelka, D. (2024), *Corona, the lockdown, and the media: a quantitative frame analysis of media coverage and restrictive policy responses*, Berlin, Boston: De Gruyter. <https://doi.org/10.1515/9783110765311>

Bollenbeck, G. (1994), *Bildung und Kultur: Glanz und Elend eines deutschen Deutungsmusters*, Frankfurt/Main: Suhrkamp.

Chari, R. and Rozas, I. (2022), *Viruses, vaccines, and antivirals: why politics matters*, Berlin, Boston: De Gruyter. <https://doi.org/10.1515/9783110743609>

Crepaz, M., Junk, W. M., Hanegraaff, M. and Berkhout, J. (2022), *Viral lobbying: strategies, access and influence during the COVID-19 pandemic*, Berlin, Boston: De Gruyter. <https://doi.org/10.1515/9783110783148>

Cooper, F., Dolezal, L., Rose, A. (2023), *COVID-19 and shame. Political emotions and public health in the UK*, London: Bloomsbury.

Feierstein, D. (2021), *Pandemia. Un balance social y político de la crisis del COVID-19*, Ciudad Autónoma de Buenos Aires: Fondo de Cultura Económica.

Fuller, T. (ed.) (1989), "THE IDEA OF A UNIVERSITY: 1950," in *The voice of liberal learning: Michael Oakeshott on education*, New Haven and London: Yale University Press, pp. 95–104.

Gallego Cuiñas, A. and Pérez Tapias, J. A. (eds.) (2022), *Pensamiento, Pandemia y Big Data: El impacto sociocultural del coronavirus en el espacio iberoamericano*, Berlin, Boston: De Gruyter.

Geuss, R. (1996), "Kultur, Bildung, Geist," *History and Theory*, 35, pp. 151–164.

Gibbs, P. (2002), "From the invisible hand to the invisible handshake – Marketing higher education," *Research in Post and Higher Education*, 7 (3), pp. 323–335.

Gibbs, P. (2011), "Finding quality in 'being good enough' conversations," *Quality in Higher Education*, 17 (2), pp. 139–150.

Gibbs, P. (2017), *Why universities should seek happiness and contentment?*, London: Bloomsbury.

Gibbs, P. (2020), "The marketingisation of higher education," in Rider, S., Peters, M. A., Hyvönen, M., Besley, T. (eds.), *World class universities. Evaluating education: normative systems and institutional practices*, Singapore: Springer.

Hemsley-Brown, J. (2011), "Market, heal thyself: The challenges of a free marketing in higher education," *Journal of Marketing for Higher Education*, 21 (2), pp. 115–132.

Kiladze, M. and Luarsabishvili, V. (2024), *The legitimization of violence. Individual, crowd and authority during the Covid-19 pandemic*, New York: Peter Lang. <https://doi.org/10.3726/b21049>

LaCapra, D. (1998), "The university in ruins?," *Critical Inquiry*, 25(1), pp. 32–55.

León, G. (2020), *Pandemia. Una historia sobre ciencia, enfermedades y el virus que cambió nuestras vidas*, Santiago de Chile: Sudamericana.

Loewe, D. (2020), *Ética y coronavirus*, Santiago de Chile: Fondo de Cultura Económica.

MacKenzie, D. (2020), *COVID-19: the pandemic that never should have happened and how to stop the next one*, New York: Hachette Books.

Masschelein, J. and Ricken, N. (2003), "Do we (still) need the concept of Bildung?," *Educational Philosophy and Theory*, 25 (2), pp. 139–154.

Mittelstrass, J. (2018), *Theoria: chapters in the philosophy of science*, Berlin: De Gruyter.

Molesworth, M., Nixon, E., and Scullion, R. (2009), "Having, being and higher education: The marketization of the university and the transformation of the student into consumer," *Teaching in Higher Education*, 14 (3), pp. 277–287.

Osterholm, M. and Olshaker, M. (2020), *La amenaza más letal. Nuestra guerra contra las pandemias y cómo evitar la próxima*, Barcelona: Editorial Planeta Chilena.

Pan, D. (1998), "The crisis of the humanities and the end of the university," *Telos*, 111, pp. 69–106.

Rallo Gruss, A. (ed.) (2022), *Arcos de Sombras*, Madrid: Dickinson.

Readings, B. (1999), *The university in ruins*, Cambridge, MA: Harvard University Press.

Schmidt, A. (2013), "Self-cultivation (*Bildung*) and sociability between mankind and the nation. Fichte and Schleiermacher on higher education," in Christopher Brooke and Elizabeth Frazer (eds.), *Ideas of Education. Philosophy and politics from Plato to Dewey*, London and New York: Routledge, pp. 160–177.

Steiner, H. and Veel, K. (2021), *Touch in the time of corona. Reflections on love, care, and vulnerability in the pandemic*, Berlin/Boston: Walter de Gruyter.

Tehranian, M. (1996), "The end of university?," *The Information Society*, 12, pp. 441–447.

Wimmer, M. (2013), "Ruins of Bildung in a knowledge society: commenting on the debate about the future of Bildung," *Educational Philosophy and Theory*, 35 (2), pp. 167–187.

# Introduction

The novel methods of teaching, along with the rapid accumulation and dissemination of research data due to swift technological development, represent a challenge for the ethical composition of modern universities. This book describes and evaluates (a) the ethical dimensions of education and research and (b) the important social function of education and research mediated by technological progress. Education and research as values with an ethical dimension are subjected to philosophical analysis. Describing the general nature of values, we investigate both education and research from a cultural perspective, followed by the detection of the role of technological progress in their realization, discussed in the corresponding sections of the book. It is argued that novel methods of education play a crucial role in the formation of its traditional social function. At the same time, modern methods of research help to elaborate diverse systems for the creation of new knowledge, determining the organization of health education and surveillance systems, among other professional advances. The role of academic citizenship in the formation of a modern civic society is also discussed. The university, as an ethically driven institution, is considered to be the main space for the self-realization of a modern professional. Only in an atmosphere of mutual respect can one expect the successful achievement of the main mission of the university—the creation of a friendly and respectful space for the self-realization of a free person.

In "The Individual and the World," John Dewey discussed the historical relation between mind and knowledge from the perspective of individualism. In the barbarian period, Dewey noted, knowledge had a divine origin that held an air of authority without leaving room for the working minds of individuals; in the medieval period, individualism became more tangible and acquired a religious character, oriented toward the salvation of an individual soul. Only in the later Middle Ages did the structure of knowledge become connected with acts performed by individuals, and hence the further relation between individual actions (including rights and duties) and the creation of knowledge.[1] Probably, this is a crossroads where, for the first time, the process of the production of knowledge (or research) became connected with the process of its transmission (or education) and dissemination (or publication), reacting against authority and aiming to acquire freedom—the possibility of critical perception of reality and the surrounding world.

Derived first from the Greek word "ethos" and later from the Latin word "mores," the basis for acting "ethically" or "morally" has meant a "custom" or a type of behavior approved by the whole family, group, tribe, class, society, or community. Different approaches explain the nature and understanding of ethical values, among which consequentialist ethics (with arguments that focus on consequences and aim for the maximization of welfare and the greatest benefits for the greatest number), communitarian ethics (taking into consideration both human responsibilities and rights, and advocating acts that are based on consensus and not on compromise), deontological ethics (focusing on duties with the leading principle of respect for other people), the "four principles approach" to ethics (focusing on beneficence, non-maleficence, respect for autonomy, and the principle of justice), narrative ethics (paying special attention to narrative in understanding situational context), and virtue ethics (embedding ethics in human character) are observable.

Ethics, by nature, is a personal phenomenon. "Personal" here means what is understood and considered to be ethical or based on an ethical basis. Individual decisions consist of preference (or choice) and action. Action is realized based on choice, which may be of different sorts: alimentary, political, religious, etc. At the moment of realization, action is personal; once realized, it leaves the domain of "personal" and forms part of the whole—of society or community—as soon as it starts sharing preferences. This is how personal ethics is realized, being transformed into a communitarian ethical phenomenon, serving not the benefit of a single human but the whole community.

Once ethics is communitarian, it determines the norms or models of behavior labeled as "ethical." This simplifies the life of society members, since in critical moments of its development, we do not need to "invent" a corresponding way of action—it is sufficient to use one of the models offered by the collective framework. Mostly, society members do not judge or criticize themselves—their behavior is correct and accepted not in a critical but in a dogmatic way. It is accepted by the majority of society, as society is based on the model of collective thinking. No room for a critical approach is left at any stage of receiving collective decisions.

But society cannot be developed in a purely collective way. Even though its members coexist inside society, for physical and mental development they still need to realize individual and not collective attempts, basic sorts of goals that cannot be reached acting together. Alimentation, orientation, reproduction, treatment, and many other personal needs are aims achieved on a personal level. Even thinking, which is an essential component that distinguishes human beings from a wide variety of animals, may not be performed on a communitarian level. Thinking may be determined, and is largely a matter of social norms, but in the concrete moment of realization, it is performed by an individual and not by the whole society. People act separately, but what keeps them together inside society is their own attempt and precaution of not violating established models of behavior in the process of social self-realization.

The attempt to form part of society and to be accepted by its members probably dates back to the remote times when the first humans realized that living together might bring prosperity. Hunting, for instance, could be more successful and less dangerous. Little by little, acting together formed some customs, and over time, customs transformed into professions, such as chief, hunter, priest, or medicine man. Priests or medicine men formed separate castes, chieftainships became hereditary, and the presence of artistic skills could also imply the separateness of some individuals from the rest of society. Probably that was the moment in the history of mankind when individuality started to originate as something distinguishable and different.[2] If society helps its members survive, it sounds logical for the latter to be content with the former. But not everything is as simple as it may seem at first sight.

"Customs" are values shared by a specific society. Culture is based on shared values, beliefs, and practices. Culture determines the ways of development for each new member of society, labeling some of them as correct and others as wrong. Any slight deviation from correctness is strictly prohibited and considered dangerous for the well-being of society. It becomes especially evident in moments of socio-political crisis or public health emergencies when, due to economic or political fluctuations, humans may rethink social norms and some may even try to escape from their realization.[3] At this moment, an intrapersonal conflict occurs when communitarian ethics cannot satisfy personal judgments. This is very exemplified first in the philosophy of Socrates and later in the philosophy of Kant, which laid the foundation for the development of individualist ethics.[4] A law should still be respected and followed but needs to be preceded by critical appraisal, neglecting its acceptance in a dogmatic way. Now, the primacy of individual thinking over the collective acceptance of reality is observable.

INTRODUCTION

Once individualism appears on the ethical scene, it starts acting against communitarian acceptance of reality. In other words, established norms are no longer considered to form an absolute truth, and the terms "truth" and "absolute" are also subjected to evaluation. This is the moment when the individual does not select the modes of acting within the bounds of existing possibilities but looks for weighty arguments to accept or reject them. The result is a conflict—a product of differently perceived reality and a distinct way of seeing the surrounding world. The differences in acting between the accepted and imagined forms of behavior are based on the ethical perception of reality.

Universities are one of the main places where ethics is formed and developed. This is due to the dual existence of ethics in everyday university life—one that considers ethics as a discipline to be discussed and studied and another that considers ethics an instrument for organizing university life.

Ethics as a discipline is offered to students of all specialties, forming part of the teaching programs of philosophy and medicine, as well as other social and biomedical disciplines. The necessity of its teaching and studying is obvious—the university is a space where methods of thinking are developed and ethical approaches to different vital situations describe the distinct ways of selecting modes of behavior, accepting some and rejecting others. The ethical perspective seems to be one of the basic platforms on which fundamental human values and rights should be placed, discussed, and subjected to critical rethinking.

Ethics as an instrument for organizing university life dates back to the period of the foundation of the first colleges and universities. This is not surprising, as the origin of the discussion regarding the relationship between science and morals dates back to Plato and Aristotle, who coined the notions of "theoretical life" and "practical life," indicating the senselessness of science once it lacks a moral orientation.[5] Traditions do not always mean high ethical standards, but they offer a period in the history of education that detects different trends in education and doctrinal attempts at forming societies. Discovering the idea of education perceived by different societies, its interpretation, and the aims of educating the youth may shed light on the role of ethics in the formation of societies.

One of the main challenges facing modern universities, especially evident from the second half of the past century, is the internationalization of education. The 20th century witnessed two large-scale and many small-scale wars, as well as armed conflicts, revolutions, and genocides. Social and political instability forced millions of people to leave their homes and move to different countries. Migration with families, especially with young family members such as schoolchildren and students, required schools and universities to create a new and friendly atmosphere based on the ethical values of interpersonal communication. Racism, xenophobia, and the inability to accept different cultures and their representatives became very evident in distinct parts of the modern world, leading to the necessity of ethical behavior for the formation of modern civic society.

However, education is not the only function of universities. Research occupies a prominent part of university life, being especially appreciated because swift technical development makes it possible to apply research results to our everyday lives. This is especially evident in the case of biomedical sciences, where new research data is immediately used to benefit modern civic society. Researchers do not work for the long run and future perspectives; their aim is to improve our lives today and tomorrow, offering new possibilities for treatment, increasing the quality of life, and creating better life expectancies. All that can comprise human happiness is wholly based on modern research in which ethics should perform a leading and determining role. Even errors committed by science frequently determine scientific development, together with discoveries, and play an important role in conditioning scientific progress.[6]

International scientific collaboration is one of the main determinants of modern research. Different stages of a research career, such as working on a PhD dissertation, conducting postdoctoral studies, or defending a habilitation thesis, frequently involve research travels to different countries. This means a meeting between distinct cultural characteristics reflected during everyday communication and forming the basis for prospective multicultural research societies. The ability to accept differences and a readiness to share values belonging to less-known cultural epistemes should be realized without experiencing fear and cultural shock toward a new and global reality.

Together with educational and research approaches, modern universities aim to introduce a social factor in community life. The feeling of belonging, of forming part of a human society that can contribute to the self-realization of its members and thus increase the index of human happiness, makes the role of ethics in building university culture understandable. From departments, offices, and classrooms, the university is converted into a cultural organism that not only shares but also creates its own values based on the principles of equality and tolerance. The core idea of modern universities is not to provide factual knowledge that in some cases can be achieved through self-education, consulting library catalogs, and downloading papers and books from electronic databases; the most important achievement of today's universities is the formation of ethically oriented responsible citizens who can create multiple and individual ways of acting during political, social, and humanitarian catastrophes based on ethical principles of behavior. Ethics, by nature, is always the ethics of the *citizen*.[7]

## INTRODUCTION

Values are basic components of cultures shared by society in specific social and temporal contexts. They are created and shared by most (universal values) or some (non-universal values) cultures. Values may be presented in the form of beliefs (religious or non-religious), actions, intentions/thoughts, and aims (individual or collective), to list just a few. All these are valuable or, at least, contain and determine the nature of something that is or should be valued. Hence the necessity of understanding cultures based on their constituting values. Being accepted in a universal way in different cultural groups, values may carry conflicting or compatible features, crucial for explaining social composition, orientation, and change.[8] The theories of Triandis (1995), which demonstrate that the dimensions of individualism and collectivism should be combined with equality or inequality in social relations; Inglehart (1998), considering that cultural change may be explained by taking into account the dimensions of materialism–post-materialism and modernization–post-modernization; Hofstede (1984), with the theory of the structure of values considering four main factors (power distance, avoiding uncertainty, masculinity/femininity, and individualism/collectivism); and Schwartz (1992), which unites six main features (values are beliefs; values refer to desirable goals; values transcend specific actions and situations; values serve as standards or criteria; values are ordered by importance; and the *relative* importance of multiple values guides actions), are recognized today as the main approaches for the study of values.

By nature, values are rather dynamic than static. Time and context not only determine the vitality of values but also condition their essence, subjecting them to severe changes or partial modifications. *Memory*, which is also a valuable phenomenon, may serve as a helpful example to demonstrate the changeable nature of values: with time, some events are kept in collective memory,[9] while others are deliberately forgotten (leading to the formation of the so-called "social amnesia"),[10] indicating the selective approach of society in composing and/or decomposing certain values that mark the specific culture. This is realized with a specific *aim* that, in turn, is a certain type of value.

*Aims* drive both thoughts and actions, on the one hand, and thoughts and actions pursue concrete *aims*, on the other. Aims form a basis for both education and research. In the first case, "An educational aim must be founded upon the intrinsic activities and needs (including original instincts and acquired habits) of the given individual to be educated,"[11] and in the second, aims help increase knowledge, determining the development of science in a non-linear manner.[12] Aims/goals and beliefs are of crucial importance for the formation of any culture, a fact taken into consideration by Schwartz while composing the well-known "Theory of Basic Values," indicating that values are beliefs and they refer to goals, transcending specific actions and being ordered by importance.[13]

The technological progress developed during the last two centuries has facilitated the process of accumulating new knowledge, on the one hand, and its dissemination, on the other, thus becoming an indispensable condition for the development of both social and biomedical sciences. Swift technological development has had, and continues to have, a significant effect on the rapid and effective creation of new knowledge, especially in the case of biomedical sciences, providing both technical facilities and better management of human resources for scientific research.[14] As noted by Fossum and Dissen regarding the hierarchical construction of living organisms, "By a series of remarkable advances in technical developments and novel discoveries during the past 50 years … we are now gaining deep insight into this organizational level."[15] Hence, there is an increased role of technological progress in understanding the surrounding world and discovering our place in it.[16] At the same time, the idea of ethical limits should be considered while articulating the role of scientific progress, as evidenced in cases of reproductive medicine and genetic engineering.[17]

It sounds paradoxical: advances in education and research do not necessarily lead to the improvement of the well-being of human society. Even more alarming is the fact that general health indicators for a major part of the world's population are gradually deteriorating. The re-emergence of diseases such as cholera and diphtheria, high incidences of hepatitis C and tuberculosis in developing countries, unsuccessful management of global pandemics such as H5N1 or COVID-19, and limited access to modern health services[18] due to poverty and social inequality necessitate a rethink of the role of universities in the modern era. One of the most important dimensions that connect the social sciences with biomedical investigation is public health.

Changing its denomination from international health to global health, the public health agenda is composed of a wide variety of modern patterns that define and describe contemporary challenges of mankind. Massive migrations intensified during the last two centuries by industrialization, globalization, and wars, as well as natural disasters and the inability to eradicate poverty, determine the further reduction of the quality of life and the shortening of the average lifespan in most of the developing world.[19] Social distancing, a sedentary lifestyle, and unhealthy diet are a few but important habits that determine the emergence of chronic diseases and the deprivation of basic mental functions. Cognitive impairment is responsible for the loss of possibilities of social self-realization and lowering self-esteem. Global mental health issues and their challenging nature, revealed in stigmatization, discrimination, social exclusion, or sexual violence toward women, are especially evident in low- and middle-income countries, among the topics illuminated in different reports from the last decade of the past century.[20] Social and cultural characteristics are altered, and their development becomes more dependent on new types of values formed as a result of community demands dictated by political, ideological, and bureaucratic frames.

Public health, as a healthcare system discipline, is supported by evidence-based biomedical research. Scientific discoveries and improvements are made by preclinical and clinical investigations with different research designs and analyzed by complex methods of statistical assessment. Research conducted at university is of particular interest, as it is a place with a wide selection of laboratorial and/or clinical facilities and research staff. University research aims not only to accumulate new data but also to transmit it to students through teaching. As the university community is based on the creation and extension of certain values admitted by all its members, university research brings into life new perspectives for investigation and founds the ways to disseminate the research data to benefit all members of both biomedical and non-biomedical society. Values as the main characteristics of modern civic society are important from both research and societal perspectives. Thus, public health research may be transformed into an effective tool to rethink the assessment of old values and the formation of new ones.

Research is very important for health communication as well: a) formative research establishes the epidemiology of the health issue, measures levels of knowledge to it and identifies the communicative channels for delivering information; b) process evaluation determines if a program is running according to plan, and c) summative evaluation measures results.[21] One of the ways of using technical facilities is developing new drugs, first testing them *in vitro*, and once being isolated and positively characterized an active component of potentially promising medication, subjecting it to further chemical elaboration and to extensive *in vitro* and *in vivo* evaluation. The complete process of preclinical and clinical drug development is almost 12 years, and it counts with the participation of researchers, government, and non-governmental organizations, as well as pharmaceutical and biotechnology companies.[22]

In the following chapters, we will demonstrate that education (or the process of transmission of knowledge) and research (or the process of production of knowledge): a) are values with an ethical dimension that should be cultivated (or created), transmitted (or taught), and disseminated (or shared), b) as values, they possess an important (social) function that is mediated by technological progress.

In Chapter 1, we will describe education from a historical perspective, briefly detecting the main historical approaches to the field in the understanding of different philosophers of education that formed distinct cultural epistemes.

In Chapter 2, we will describe education as part of university system and analyze the role of ethics in education, considering education as a valuable phenomenon and offering a description of the role of modern technologies in education.

In Chapter 3, we will describe research as part of educational systems, making a special emphasis on the different historical traditions of hosting science in different parts of the world; again, the role of ethics in research will be analyzed, followed by the discussion of research as a valuable phenomenon and by the role of modern technologies in research.

In Chapter 4, we will explore the modern structure of universities, highlighting their potential contributions to enhancing both teaching and research. Additionally, we will delve into the pivotal role universities play in conducting public health research, shedding light on their impact on societal well-being.

Chapter 5 will provide an analysis of our firsthand experience in teaching and conducting research at various Georgian universities. This chapter aims to offer valuable insights into the unique challenges, opportunities, and dynamics observed within the educational and research landscape of Georgia.

Chapter 6 will overview the notion of "happiness" from historical and educational perspectives.

Finally, Chapter 7 will present the overarching conclusions drawn from the book. These conclusions will synthesize the key findings and perspectives discussed throughout the chapters, providing readers with a comprehensive understanding of the themes explored in the context of education, research, and their ethical dimensions in the modern university setting.

## Notes

1. Dewey, 1916a, pp. 301–302.
2. Dewey, 1916b; Russell, 2010.
3. Hogan, 2019; Collier and Collier, 1991; Soifer, 2012; Kananovich, 2021.
4. Aranguren, 1968.
5. Mittelstrass, 2018, p. 147.
6. Ibid., p. 25.
7. Ibid., p. 152.
8. Weber, 1958; Durkheim, 1964.
9. Billig, 1990; Kattago, 2001; Schmitt, 2016.
10. Passerini, 2005.
11. Dewey, 1916c, p. 114.

INTRODUCTION

12. Kuhn, 1969.
13. Schwartz, 1992.
14. In a speech pronounced on June 26, 2000, announcing the human genome draft sequence, F. Collins stated: "In the 1980s, trying to track down the cystic fibrosis gene took us about 10 years of very hard work. There were probably 100 researchers involved and millions of dollars were spent. With the database that's now available an average post-doc working in a good lab would be able to accomplish that in a couple of weeks" (Fossum and Dissen, 2007, p. 195).
15. Ibid., pp. 161–162.
16. At the same time, the dependence on technical equipment and additional human assistance deprive a man of science of independence in his decisions and views, making him clearly biased in the government's (or donor's) favor: "The rise of men of science to great eminence in the State is a modern phenomenon. Scientists, like other innovators, had to fight for recognition: some were banished; some were burnt; some were kept in dungeons; others merely had their books burnt; But gradually it came to be realized that they could put power into the hands of the State. [...] The scientists of the past did their work very largely as individuals, but the scientist of our day needs enormously expensive equipment and a laboratory with many assistants. All this he can obtain through the favor of the government, or, in America, of very rich men. He is thus no longer an independent worker, but essentially part and parcel of some large organization. [...] Most research requires expensive apparatus; some kinds require the financing of expeditions to different regions. Without facilities provided by a government or a university, few men can achieve much in modern science. The conditions which determine who is to have access to such facilities are therefore of great importance. If only those are eligible who are considered orthodox in current controversies, scientific progress will soon cease, and will give way to a scholastic reign of authority such as stifled throughout the Middle Ages" (Russell, 2010, pp. 32, 36, 65).
17. On this topic see Mittelstrass, 1999, 2018. Regarding genetic tests: "It is stated that when a genetic test is of known predictive value or gives reliable information about a known heritable condition, samples must be anonymized before testing. Where the research requires the use of identifiable individuals and involves tests of known clinical or predictive value, explicit consent should be obtained and participant should be given the option of whether to know the result" (Brannan et al., 2012, pp. 620–621).
18. More than 9 million children's death worldwide is preventable due to warranting the access to basic medicines and vaccines. Among the difficulties

leading to coverage of medicines in community health insurance are lack of infrastructure, less developed drug supply systems and non-sufficient political support (Quick and Moore, 2010).

19. As it is noted, "[…] living past the age of 60 is not the norm in 45 out of 195 countries (WHO, 2006). The inequality is most pronounced among the mail population—life expectancy at birth for males in 55 countries is 60 or less. The risk of dying at a very early age is higher today compared to almost 50 years ago among the poorest countries" (Friel and Marmot, 2010, p. 65).
20. Patel et al., 2010.
21. Bertrand et al., 2011.
22. Freire, 2011.

## Bibliography

Aranguren, J. L. L. (1968), *Ética y Política*, Madrid: Ediciones Guadarrama.

Bertrand, J. T., Payne Merritt, A., and Saffitz, G. (2011), "Health communication: a catalyst to behaviour change," in R. Parker and M. Sommer (eds.), *Routledge handbook of global public health*. 1st edition. London and New York: Routledge, pp. 313–325.

Billig, M. (1990), "Collective memory, ideology, and the British royal family," in D. Middleton and D. Edwards (eds.), *Collective remembering*, London: Sage Publications, pp. 60–80.

Brannan, S., Chrispin, E., Davies, M., English, V., Mussell, R., Sheather, J. and Sommerville, A. (2012), *Medical ethics today: The BMA's handbook of ethics and law*. 3rd edition. Oxford: Blackwell Publishing.

Collier, R. B. and Collier, D. (1991), *Shaping the political arena: critical junctures, the labor movement, and regime dynamics in Latin America*, Princeton: Princeton University Press.

Dewey, J. (1916a), "The individual and the world," in J. Dewey, *Democracy and education, the middle works 1899–1924, vol. 9*, Carbondale: Southern Illinois University Press, pp. 300–315.

Dewey, J. (1916b), *Ethics, the middle works 1899–1924, vol. 5*, Carbondale: Southern Illinois University Press.

Dewey, J. (1916c), "Aims in education," in J. Dewey, *Democracy and education, the middle works 1899–1924, vol. 9*, Carbondale: Southern Illinois University Press, pp. 107–117.

Durkheim, E. (1964), *Suicide*, Glencoe, Il: Free Press.

Fossum, S. and Dissen, E. (2007), "Methods in molecular biology," in P. Laake, H. Breinen Benestad and B. R. Olsen (eds.), *Research methodology in the medical and biological sciences*, Amsterdam: Elsevier, pp. 161–197.

Freire, M. C. (2011), "Developing drugs for the developing world. The role of product development partnerships," in R. Parker and M. Sommer (eds.), *Routledge handbook of global public health*. 1st edition. London and New York: Routledge, pp. 490–496.

Friel, S. and Marmot, M. (2010), "Global health inequalities. Structures, power, and social distribution of health," in Richard Parker and Marni Sommer (eds.), *Routledge handbook of global public health*. 1st edition. London and New York: Routledge, pp. 65–79.

Hofstede, G., (1984), *Culture's consequences: international differences in work-related values*, Beverly Hills, CA: Sage Publications.

Hogan, J. (2019), "The critical juncture concept's evolving capacity to explain policy change," *European Policy Analysis*, 5(2), pp. 170–189.

Inglehart, R., (1998), *Modernización y Postmodernización: El cambio cultural, económico y político en 43 sociedades*, Madrid: CIS.

Kananovich, V. (2021), "#presidentspartingwords at a Critical Juncture: Reclaiming the Autonomous Subject in Social Media Discourse on Coronavirus in Belarus," *Journal of Communication Inquiry*, 46, pp. 244–267.

Kattago, S. (2001), *Ambiguous memory: The Nazi past and German national identity*, Westport, Conn.: Praeger.

Kuhn, T. S. (1969), *The structure of scientific revolutions*, Chicago: University of Chicago Press.

Lorenz, K. (2002), *On aggression*, London and New York: Routledge.

Mittelstrass, J. (1999), "The impact of the new biology on ethics," *European Review: Interdisciplinary Journal of the Academia Europea*, 7, pp. 277–283.

Mittelstrass, J. (2018), *Theoria: chapters in the philosophy of science*, Berlin: De Gruyter.

Passerini, L. (2005), *Memory and totalitarianism*, London and New York: Routledge.

Patel, V., Koschorke, M., and Prince, M. (2010), "Closing the treatment gap for mental disorders," in Richard Parker and Marni Sommer (eds.)., *Routledge Handbook of global public health*. 1st edition. London and New York: Routledge, pp. 385–393.

Quick, J. D. and Moore, E. O. (2010), "Global access to essential medicines. Past, present, and future," in Richard Parker and Marni Sommer (eds.),

*Routledge handbook of global public health.* 1st edition. London and New York: Routledge, pp. 421–432.

Russell, B. (2010), "The role of individuality," in Bertrand Russell, *Authority and the individual*, London and New York: Routledge, pp. 27–39.

Schmitt, J.-C. (2016), "Images and the work of memory, with special reference to the six-century mosaics of Ravenna, Italy," in Elma Brenner, Meredith Cohen, Mary Franklin-Brown (eds.), *Memory and Commemoration in Medieval Culture*, London and New York: Routledge, pp. 14–32.

Schwartz, S. (1992), "Universals in the content and structure of values: theory and empirical tests in 20 countries," in Mark Zanna (ed.), *Advances in experimental social psychology*, New York: Academic Press, pp. 1–65.

Soifer, H. D. (2012), "The causal logic of critical junctures," *Comparative Political Studies*, 45(12), pp. 1572–1597.

Triandis, H. (1995), *Individualism and collectivism*, Boulder, CO: Westview Press.

Weber, M. (1958), *The Protestant ethic and the spirit of capitalism*, New York: Scribner's.

CHAPTER 1

# Historical Background

## 1.1. Introduction

This chapter attempts to link the main peculiarities of education as detected and characterized by representatives of distinct cultural epistemes. In particular, we shall briefly discuss the general approaches to education formulated by Johann Heinrich Pestalozzi (as a Swiss educational reformer), Friedrich Froebel (as a German educational reformer), John Dewey (as a representative of the American pragmatist educational system), Miguel de Unamuno and Ortega y Gasset (as representatives of the Spanish educational system), Paul Natorp (as a representative of neo-Kantian approaches in pedagogy), Maria Montessori (the creator of the "Montessori method"), Jean Piaget (as an author who connected epistemology with psychology), and Bertrand Russell (as a representative of the British educational system).

### 1.1.1. Some Preliminary Ideas

Arguably, three basic philosophers that may serve as reference points for the further development of innovative educational thought in Europe and the United States are Jean-Jacques Rousseau, Immanuel Kant, and Hegel. Their ideas, representing many similarities and certain differences in approaches, helped create a solid foundation for the understanding of education generally and its social aspect particularly.

Rousseau's impact on education and the development of thinking, in general, is of historical importance. He contributed to the formation of romantic culture and revolutionary aesthetics in France, which, globally speaking, led to new directions in educational thought in Europe. His educational approach was child-centered, emphasizing the child rather than the material being taught, and influenced educational ideas for the next two centuries. Rousseau argued against the idea that society is essential for the happiness of an individual, instead proposing that society creates additional obstacles for humans, preventing them from feeling happy. According to Rousseau, the goal of education is to achieve a state of nature in which individuals can be satisfied with their basic needs and avoid injustice and oppression.[1]

Kant, greatly interested in Rousseau's ideas, particularly focused on the adverse effects that society may have on humans, aligning with Rousseau's concerns about the evils of society. However, Kant could not accept the idea of a pre-rational existence of mankind, emphasizing the need for education to develop rationality in individuals. Only through education can individuals achieve autonomy and define themselves as human beings.[2]

Hegel, while agreeing with Kant's criticism of Rousseau's state of nature, opposed Kant's understanding of morality and justice. He believed that human happiness is realized in society, which forms good citizens and a just state. Hegel did not see any divergence between individual and common goals and argued that freedom should be imposed upon individuals by parents and teachers to create educated individuals who know themselves and are not dictated by force or natural conditions.[3]

### 1.1.1.1. *Sozialpädagogik* and Individual Ethics and Psychology: Natorp and Herbart

To explore two basic foundations of modern educational theory, we need to distinguish between different approaches to understanding the term. On the one hand, we have the so-called *Sozialpädagogik*, formed by Paul Natorp, and on the other hand, the role of individual ethics and psychology, founded by Johann Friedrich Herbart. Although the philosophers discussed in this chapter seem to align more with Natorp's ideas, the ethical side of *Sozialpädagogik* connects various educational approaches to Herbart's ideas.

The basic idea of *Sozialpädagogik* focuses on communities, emphasizing the connection between youth and popular education as an educational project. Natorp believed that education could solve emerging social difficulties and transform into a universal instrument for social well-being.

In contrast, Herbart emphasized individuality in education, focusing on the development of a child's character and personal talents. He is considered the "father of modern science of education," as he introduced education to universities as a discipline, formulated instructional methodology based on psychological approaches, and defined the goal of education as the development of moral character.[4]

In the following sections, we shall explore how similar educational approaches have developed in different cultural epistemes and their role in shaping educational systems from historical, philosophical, and educational perspectives.

*1.1.1.1.1. Johann Heinrich Pestalozzi*

Pestalozzi was among the philosophers of education who strongly influenced the transformation of educational approaches, modifying the understanding of teaching in different countries worldwide.[5] Perhaps most convincing in Pestalozzi's approaches was his application of theoretical ideas into practice, operating schools in Neuhof, Stans, Burgdorf, and Yverdon, where he demonstrated the practical benefits of comprehensive educational approaches.

Developing the "heart, hands, and head" method, Pestalozzi introduced a threefold approach to education, focusing on the development of rationality, skills, and emotional understanding of the surrounding world. His methodological instruments, explained in books such as *Leonard and Gertrude* and *How Gertrude Teaches Her Children*, facilitated the spread of ideas regarding the reasons and benefits of education. In 1951, the Philosophical Library published a collection of Pestalozzi's aphorisms.[7]

Joseph Neef and other authors further spread Pestalozzi's teaching approaches, making him famous in the United States. Other authors who propagated his ideas included H. Mann[8] and H. Bernard.[9] Edward A. Sheldon's version of Pestalozzi's ideas became known as the Oswego method, and John Dewey was also strongly influenced by Pestalozzi.[10]

1.1.1.1.1.1. PESTALOZZI'S METHOD

Pestalozzi elaborated his famous approach to education, called the "method," focusing on the training of teachers and the formation of citizens, thereby determining the social function of education. He emphasized the necessity of understanding the natural possibilities of a child and the circumstances of the surrounding world to develop in children a harmonious feeling of inner satisfaction based on the development of individual creative possibilities. According to Pestalozzi, the development of these possibilities depends on the concrete social and historical context, emphasizing creative impulses over factual knowledge in the formation of a citizen.[11]

*1.1.1.1.2. Friedrich Froebel*

Arguing for the importance of preschool education and coining the term *kindergarten*, Friedrich Froebel was one of the most influential philosophers of education not only in Germany but also abroad.[12] Froebel introduced a female factor in education, organizing special training courses for women teachers, opening doors to a new profession for them.[13] Froebel's first university years were spent at the University of Jena, followed by practical experience, both institutional and private. He first worked at the "Model School" established by Pestalozzi's disciple Gottlieb Gruner, followed by a visit to Yverdon, where Froebel met Pestalozzi and felt the necessity of developing Pestalozzi's and Rousseau's ideas in a more systematic way. This goal he achieved after returning to the "Model School" and second, through private tutoring of Baron von Holzhausen's sons, including their two-year visit to the Yverdon school. Institutional and personal educational experiences brought Froebel back to university education. He studied first at the University of Göttingen and later at the University of Berlin, where he learned languages, mineralogy, history, chemistry, physics, and crystallography. These studies were interrupted by voluntary military service, followed later by university years, assisting Professor Christian Weiss at the University of Berlin. The year 1816 marked the beginning of Froebel's professional career.

### 1.1.1.1.2.1. KINDERGARTEN AND SPIELGABEN

In the village of Griesheim, Froebel founded a school called the "Universal German Educational Institute," which moved after a year to the village of Kielhau, where the number of pupils reached 56. It was in Kielhau where Froebel published his work "The Education of Man," elucidating the principle of wholeness, emphasizing the connection between school and life based on the ideas of Rousseau and Froebel's modern German philosophy. Due to negative reception by Prussian authorities, the school suffered a financial crisis that forced Froebel to move to Switzerland and found new schools, first in Wartensee and later in Willisau. Again, Froebel's liberal ideas faced opposition, this time from Jesuit clergy, prompting him to move to Burgdorf and become director of an orphanage previously supervised by Pestalozzi. Returning to Germany in 1836, Froebel established the first early childhood educational institution called the "Play and Activity Institute." In 1844, he published "Mother-, Play-, and Nursery Songs," followed by his theory of "gifts" (*Spielgaben*) a year later. Froebel theorized the use of simple wooden toys and soft balls—representing the six colors of the rainbow—or three elemental forms (a hard ball, a cube, and a cylinder) symbolizing movement and stillness, as tools for educational practice. Among other educational instruments were slats and sticks, and among activities were drawing and sewing, to name just a few. Although Froebel is not considered a philosopher who formed a systematic form of thinking, his approach to education represents the relevance of humanistic aims, laying a firm basis for the development of the philosophy of education.[14]

*1.1.1.1.3. John Dewey*
John Dewey's views on education played a crucial role in the development of pedagogy worldwide. Writing on the problems of education in both school and university systems, Dewey offered a systematic approach to the topic, indicating weaknesses in the discipline and noting possible ways of improving the situation. Professional ethics, academic freedom, and a philosophical understanding of education were central themes in his work. Dewey's educational legacy can be categorized into three basic directions: (a) his contribution to the development of different disciplines,[15] (b) the reception of his philosophy of education in different countries,[16] and (c) the intersections between his ideas and those of other philosophers.[17] Additionally, we recommend the informative bibliographical article by Paciano Fermoso Estébanez, which lists Dewey's main works dedicated to educational questions. Fermoso Estébanez divides Dewey's works on education into principal philosophical works (general considerations) and pedagogical thought and philosophical-educational works.[18]

1.1.1.1.3.1. DEMOCRACY AND EDUCATION
In his famous work *Democracy and Education* Dewey emphasizes the aims of education. After recognizing that "education as such has no aims"[19] and offering the term "suggestions to educators"[20] in place of aims, Dewey lists some main approaches to a productive educational system.[21] Here, the focus is on understanding the aim of education as the method of cooperation between a teacher and an individual to be educated. Emphasis is placed on discovering one's capacities through the construction of procedures, which in turn test the aims.[22] This educational system is oriented toward the individual, helping them recognize their personal possibilities, which ultimately lead to freedom.[23] A critical approach aids in developing the ability to start thinking, thereby converting intelligent activity into a method. Dewey characterizes the role of educators as protectors against the generalization of ideas that may easily become abstract, detached from concrete contexts.[24] According to Dewey, both teaching and learning should not be mere means; they should have their own immediate products. Teaching is not merely an empty technique that forms the specialty of pedagogy, as such specialties cannot create free nations aware of their freedom.[25] The only theories useful in education are personal theories, generated and tested individually. Self-understanding is the only way to escape from dogmas and seek or attempt to understand the truth.[26]

*1.1.1.1.4. Miguel de Unamuno*
The vast bibliography on education in the case of Unamuno may be divided into three parts: first, reflecting the social and educational thoughts of the author;[27]

second, describing Unamuno's ideas concerning education in general;[28] and third, presenting Unamuno as an intellectual related to the university.[29] This division of critical bibliography seems logical, as Unamuno broadly published on the three mentioned topics. On the scene of education, Unamuno acted from a double perspective: as an intellectual and as a professional in the field.[30] Being a prominent writer and public figure, the Basque philosopher dedicated separate essays[31] and multiple discussions in general texts[32] to the topic.

#### 1.1.1.1.4.1. An Idea of Education

In specialized literature, it is admitted that Unamuno did not form any system of philosophical thought. Julián Marías, in his books,[33] noted that despite the fact that Unamuno developed philosophical thought in Spain, he was not a professional philosopher, and his legacy is "a serious problem of philosophy." Gómez de la Torre (2000), Ciriaco Morón Arroyo (2003), Joaquín Madruga Méndez (2007) and Maraco Santos (2018) agree that Unamuno's essayistic work is of an unsystematic nature. The question described here, education, was understood in a similar manner—Unamuno tried to explain his ideas concerning pedagogy in his peculiar manner of polarizing original ideas, enriching them with individual professional experience. His essay titled "On the Teaching of Classicism" ("Sobre la enseñanza del clasicismo") describes Unamuno's theory in practice. His main professional challenge was to fill the educational process with curiosity, making individuals inquisitive about new knowledge. According to Unamuno, the main idea of education is to make an individual free and non-dependent on prearranged scholastic schemes. Hence, the necessity for a teacher/professor to interface without any defined program of education. This makes it necessary to rethink the role of the teacher in education, relating it to traditional and dogmatic approaches to pedagogy.[34] Thus, pedagogy is converted from a profession into philosophy, less dependent on technical development and aiming at the formation of free men.[35] If the main goal of education is to form free individuals, this must be realized by taking into consideration the role of an individual in society and his basic human rights, as outlined in the essay "Separatist Nationalism" ("Nacionalismo separatista").[36] The aim of education, according to Unamuno, is to help an individual find his place in the surrounding world, to realize his possibilities. According to this scheme, the person is not the product of the epoch or of determined borders but of his proper possibilities.[37] Unamuno's approach to truth is that questioning is the only way for understanding.[38]

#### 1.1.1.1.4.2. Pestalozzi, Dewey, and Unamuno: Comparative Remarks

Colvin and King have summarized the coincidences in Pestalozzi's and Dewey's approaches to education. In particular, the authors collect the common themes into the following groups: understanding education as the method of trial and error,[39] accepting the school as the mode of the creation and building of life, introducing, along with the school subjects, lessons on drawing, writing, and physical development,[40] understanding the family as a model for school,[41] teaching concrete topics instead of abstracting the knowledge,[42] detecting the concept of "universal educability,"[43] and appealing to student interests and individualization.[44]

Another interesting topic is to formulate some final conclusions on the similarity of educational approaches proposed by John Dewey and Miguel de Unamuno. What is apparent for us is the relation between *education* and *individual approaches* on the one hand and the formation of a *free individual* as the main goal of education on the other. To be more illustrative, we will summarize Dewey's and Unamuno's ideas as a unique educational system, which carries the main goal of individual liberation through education.

There is no doubt that the accumulation of knowledge results in a deeper understanding of proper possibilities. The latter is an instrument for discovering the truth that can help an individual to create and share values in society. Dewey noted that: "It is no accident that the terms communication and community lie so near together; or that intercourse means equally speech and any intimate mode of associated life."[45] As Unamuno put it, discovering truth is the equivalent of rejecting dogmas, of trying to reach with proper mental possibilities the answers to the main questions of existence. This is the way of understanding life that makes a man free. Mental operation, and not technical progress, is the instrument for self-recognition. That is why the role of the individual is prominent and decisive, and each citizen is equally important for society. To the mentioned, Dewey adds the importance of a special ambiance that will help the individual to reveal and develop personal skills. Moreover, Unamuno's *questioning* is the same phenomenon as Dewey's thinking, as the "method of intelligent learning." The role of the teacher, thus, is to stimulate thinking, not to drown into pedagogical schemes and pure technical approaches (Unamuno), and not to draw the ends of general and ultimate nature (Dewey).

Unamuno and Dewey coincide in the will to help the individual develop personal skills, to ask questions to approximate himself to the metaphysical truth. The main idea of education, thus, seems to be the development of personality, learning by questioning, ignoring dogmas, and the apparent reality that rests on the surface of common things. In this case, the role of the mind is decisive, and the critical approach to education and self-understanding is achieved.

Pestalozzi's, Unamuno's, and Dewey's educational approaches should be considered as a reflection based on the development of their contemporary educational systems. Naturally, after almost a century, these opinions need to be adjusted to our contemporary views of pedagogy and the building of civic society. However, what makes their ideas vivid and still progressive is the method of placing the individual at the center of the pedagogical process, arming him with education as the main instrument to protect against society.

### 1.1.1.1.5. *Ortega y Gasset*

The fact that Ortega y Gasset never considered himself to be a philosopher of education, and the relatively small number of pedagogical texts in his complete works, have led to the formation of a view in specialized literature that Ortega was not an educator in the classical understanding of the term. However, upon deeper examination of some of his famous texts, one can discover scientific approaches to pedagogy, as well as its philosophical and anthropological foundations, including social aspects and the role of the university in the process of education.[46]

#### 1.1.1.1.5.1. EDUCATION, CULTURE, AND CIRCUMSTANCES

According to Ortega, pedagogy belongs to the realm of human acts that transform existing reality. He compares pedagogy to physics and notes that just as the former tries to define the laws of nature, the latter anticipates the essence of man and seeks instruments to shape a person according to what they should be. Based on the ideas of Johann Friedrich Herbart, whom Ortega considered the first educator to systematize the basic questions of pedagogy, Ortega relates education to science, concluding that philosophy should be studied by educators since pedagogy applies problems of education through thought and feelings. Ortega does not consider man to be merely a biological creature; physiology is only a pretext for one's existence. Hence, the appearance of a social aspect of pedagogy in Ortega's thought became very evident after his travels to Germany.

According to Ortega, science, morality, and art are specifically human acts; being human means participation in the development of all three spheres. The greater our participation, the more human our existence, as an isolated individual cannot truly be human, noted Ortega, making references to Natorp's thought and comparing a solitary individual to an abstraction, understanding human reality in communication with others. Hence, the basic principles offered by Ortega include the deepening of the social dimension of education, understanding the ethical value of social pedagogy, and the necessity of establishing secular schools.[47]

### 1.1.1.1.6. *Paul Natorp*

The ideas that stimulated Natorp's pedagogical thought emerged from various readings, born of reflection on Pestalozzi's method and a critical uptake of Herbart's model of teaching. Natorp's innovative ideas strongly influenced the formation of philosophical approaches later realized by Edmund Husserl, Ernst

Cassirer, Nicolai Hartmann, and Martin Heidegger. Noteworthy is Natorp's approach to education as a child's own creative work, realized during different school activities, and his recognition of the role of work as a basic aspect of human social interaction.[48] Neo-Kantian philosophy served as a basis for Natorp's approaches to education. Together with Herman Cohen, who supervised his habilitation thesis, Natorp is considered one of the most prominent figures of the so-called Marburg School of German Neo-Kantianism.[49] Influenced by Plato's[50] and Pestalozzi's[51] ideas and discussing social, political, and cultural aspects of education, Natorp considered necessary the formation of a community based on principles of justice and democracy.

#### 1.1.1.1.6.1. EDUCATION AS A SCIENTIFIC DISCIPLINE

Natorp considered it necessary to study human consciousness to understand the basis of social patterns of education. He considered pedagogy from epistemological, moral, and political perspectives, leading to the foundation of critical pedagogy. According to Natorp, community and education are so intrinsically linked that one cannot exist without the other. What shapes a person is the understanding of their social basis, the ideas they carry, and the ideals they follow. Hence, Natorp emphasized the necessity of approaching education from a social perspective, with social education being the only possible type of education. Natorp distinguished the role of language in the development of interpersonal relations from ethical and aesthetic perspectives, indicating the mediating role that language plays in the formation of cultural traditions. Language represents an imperfect way of cultural objectification, and *speaking* is an act that lays a firm foundation for social communication established between children when they play. Thus, playing, as well as other spontaneous acts, should be transformed into educational instruments that will result in building communication from the "bottom-up" rather than "top-down."[52]

##### 1.1.1.1.6.1.1. *Natorp and Dewey: Comparative Remarks*

In an interesting article dedicated to investigating comparative aspects that formed Paul Natorp's, John Dewey's, and Sergius Hessen's pedagogical systems,[53] Wojciech Hanuszkiewicz indicates the existence of the so-called "concept of pedagogy as an applied philosophy," introduced by Hessen and evident, according to him, in the works of Natorp and Dewey. At the same time, Hessen noted that Dewey's approach differs from his proper, as well as from Natorp's understandings of the notion, that is revealed in reflection on the static concept of the opposition between values and facts. Although both Natorp and Dewey rejected the static concept of the opposition between values and facts, Dewey's position differs in the moment of treating the idea of eternity, refusing to accept it due to its perception in a static structure.[54]

### 1.1.1.1.7. Maria Montessori

Born in Italy on August 31, 1870, Maria Montessori studied medicine, becoming the first female medical student in the country. Her first professional experience involved working with mentally retarded children at the Psychiatric Clinic of the University of Rome. Influenced by the writings of Édouard Séguin and his teacher, Dr. Jean Marc Gaspard Itard, Montessori discovered a new pedagogical approach to treating retardation, which replaced the medical approach. Her innovative educational methods were initially applied to treat children at the newly founded Orthophrenic School. This experience proved successful and was later extended when Montessori began working with healthy children. She used three-dimensional shapes and objects of different colors and shapes in the newly established Casa dei Bambini. Her educational approach was highly successful, leading to the creation of a special training course and the publication of her work titled *The Montessori Method*. Soon, her method was adopted not only in Italy but also in Switzerland and later expanded to model schools in various countries including England, China, India, Mexico, Argentina, and America.

#### 1.1.1.1.7.1. THE MONTESSORI METHOD

Montessori identified sensitive periods in a child's development responsible for language acquisition, grammar skills, and the understanding of order and refinement of senses. She delineated several stages of child development: the "stage of the absorbent mind," lasting the first six years of life, characterized by observation, experimentation, and interaction with the surroundings; the second stage, from 6 to 12 years, focused on the understanding of moral consciousness; and the third stage, from 12 to 18 years, marked by the transition from puberty to adolescence. Montessori's philosophy is considered a philosophy of early childhood education, transcending cultural boundaries.[55] Another aspect of Montessori's educational philosophy was the role of the teacher, who served as a facilitator rather than an authority figure, creating an environment in which children could teach themselves.[56]

### 1.1.1.1.8. Jean Piaget

Born in Switzerland on August 9, 1896, Jean Piaget graduated from the University of Neuchâtel and conducted research at psychological laboratories in Zurich before moving to Paris to work with schoolchildren. In Paris, Piaget developed the "clinical-interview method," focusing on children's responses to discover their reasoning processes. He linked the study of knowledge with psychology, viewing learning as an active process leading to cognitive development.[57]

#### 1.1.1.1.8.1. Assimilation, Accommodation, Equilibration

Piaget proposed that successful learning relies on the processes of assimilation, accommodation, and equilibration. Assimilation involves receiving information through the senses and comparing it with existing mental representations. If the information is new, new schemas are created to accommodate it. This process leads to cognitive growth through either adaptation or the creation of new schemas, resulting in equilibration. Piaget identified three types of knowledge: physical, social, and logico-mathematical. He advocated for teaching practices that align with children's understanding of the world and emphasized individualized approaches to education.

### *1.1.1.1.9. Bertrand Russell*

Russell was a key figure in the philosophy of education, formulating ideas systematically and addressing education at all stages: preschool, school, and university. He focused on the development of human character, aligning his ideas with those of German educational philosophers.

#### 1.1.1.1.7.1. On Education

In his work *On Education*,[58] first published in 1926, Russell outlined the aims of education and provided a historical overview of educational approaches in Athens, China, Japan, Britain, and America. He rejected gender distinctions in excellence and identified four basic characteristics essential for ideal character: vitality, courage, sensitivity, and intelligence. Russell emphasized the importance of character education, discussing topics such as constructiveness, truthfulness, affection, and sympathy. He underscored the significance of love in acquiring knowledge, stating that a lack of love impedes the acquisition of knowledge. Russell advocated for viewing knowledge not as a task but as a source of joy, enabling individuals to overcome destructive passions.

## Notes

1. Rousseau, 1987.
2. Kant, 1960, 1996a, 1996b, 1996c, 2001, 2007a, 2007b.
3. Hegel, 1991.
4. On Herbart, see Schmitz, 1964; Wolman, 1968; Dunken, 1969; Blyth, 1981; Pettoello, 1988; Hilgenheger, 1993; De Garmo, 2001; by Herbart, see Herbart, 1982a, 1982b, 1982c.

5. For Pestalozzi's educational approaches from historical and modern perspectives, see the papers of Rebekka Horlacher (2013a, 2013b, 2019).
6. Pestalozzi, 1801/1900, 1801/1906.
7. *The Education of Man: Aphorisms.*
8. Mann, 1846.
9. Barnard, 1906.
10. Colvin and King, 2018.
11. Pestalozzi, 1998.
12. Valkanova and Brehony, 2006; Gomez Ferreira et al., 2019.
13. Read, 2003.
14. Weston, 1998.
15. Cadrecha Caparros, 1990; Catalán, 1991, 2001; Kennedy, 2006; González Hernández, 2011; Santos Gómez, 2011; Rosales, 2012; Sotelino Losada, 2015; Carreras Planas, 2015; Skowroński, 2016; Vaamonde Gamo and Nubiola, 2016; Esteban, 2017.
16. Fernandes de Andrade and Vinicius da Cunha, 2016; Miovska-Spaseva, 2016; Rogacheva, 2016; Fenyő, 2016.
17. Rubin, 2010; Cláudio Matos, 2011; Pallarès Piquer and Muñoz Escalada, 2017; Luarsabishvili, 2019.
18. Fermoso Estébanez, 1991; Zorić, 2016; Taylor Xóchil and Padilla, 2016.
19. Dewey, 1916, p. 114.
20. Ibidem.
21. According to him: "An aim must be capable of translation into a method of cooperating with the activities of those undergoing instruction. It must suggest the kind of environment needed to deliberate and to organize *their* capacities. Unless it lends itself to the construction of specific procedures, and unless these procedures test, correct, and amplify the aims, the latter is worthless. Instead of helping the specific task of teaching, it prevents the use of ordinary judgment in observing and sizing up the situation. It operates to exclude recognition of everything except what squares up with the fixed end in view." (Ibid., p. 115).
22. This is the critical approach to education, which was considered by Unamuno anti-dogmatic and of a humanistic nature (Unamuno, *Obras completas* VIII, 1970, p. 514).
23. Dewey insists that "The sole direct path to enduring improvement in the methods of instruction and learning consists in centring upon the conditions

which exact, promote, and test thinking. Thinking *is* the method of intelligent learning, of learning that employs and rewards mind" (Dewey, "Education as necessity," 1916, p. 159).

24. "Educators have to be on their guard against ends that are alleged to be general and ultimate. Every activity, however specific, is, of course, general in its ramified connections, for it leads out indefinitely into other things. So far as a general idea makes us more alive to these connections, it cannot be too general. But 'general' also means 'abstract,' or detached from all specific context. And such abstractness means remoteness, and throws us back, once more, upon teaching and learning as mere means of getting ready for an end disconnected from the means. That education is literally and all the time its own reward means that no alleged study or discipline is educative unless it is worthwhile in its own immediate having. A truly general aim broadens the outlook; it stimulates one to take more consequences (connections) into account. This means a wider and more flexible observation of means." (Dewey, "Education as necessity," 1916, p. 116).

25. Dewey recognizes that "An individual must actually try, in play or work, to do something with material in carrying out his own impulsive activity, and then note the interaction of his energy and that of the material employed." Thus, pedagogy is not a form of technology; it is a way of mental creation and recreation that considers education as instrument for understanding the surrounded world (Dewey, "Education as necessity," 1916, p. 160).

26. As Dewey put it, "Men must observe for themselves, and form their own theories and personally test them. Such a method was the only alternative to the imposition of dogma as truth, a procedure which reduced mind to the formal act of acquiescing in truth" (Dewey, "Education as necessity," 1916, p. 303).

27. Herrero Castro, 1991; Morón Arroyo, 2003; Gordo Piñar, 2012.

28. Aguilera Aguilera, 1965; Buonaventura Delgado, 1973; Gómez Molleda, 1986; Rubio Latorre, 1974; Barros Dias, 1994; Blanco Prieto, 2011.

29. García Blanco, 1963; Gómez Molleda, 1963, 1986; Berdugo Gómez de la Torre, 2000; Madruga Méndez, 2005.

30. *De mi vida*, Madrid: Espasa-Calpe, 1979.

31. "Otro arabesco pedagógico," in Miguel de Unamuno, *Obras completas*, Madrid: Esceliser, 1966; "Mas sobre los pedagogos," in Miguel de Unamuno, *Obras completas*, Madrid: Esceliser, 1970; "El día de la infancia," in Miguel de Unamuno, *Obras completas*, Madrid: Esceliser, 1970.

32. *Paz en la Guerra*, Madrid: Espasa-Calpe, 1964; *Epistolario inédito I (1894–1914)*. Ed. by L. Robles. Madrid: Espasa-Calpe, 1991; *Amor y pedagogía*, Madrid: Alianza, 1997.

33. Marías, 1953, 1967.
34. Unamuno, 1970, p. 514.
35. Ibidem, pp. 1329–1330.
36. Ibidem, p. 629.
37. Múgica, 1909, p. 236.
38. Unamuno, 1973, p. 14.
39. Both educators ran experimental/laboratory schools and believed in the importance of training in the professional development of teachers. In Pestalozzi's case, see Barlow, 1977.
40. Dewey and Dewey, 1915/2016.
41. The creation of family atmosphere in school was decisive for Pestalozzi and Dewey argued that school should be organized using a family as a model (Dewey, 1899/1915).
42. Pestalozzi, 1801/1900; Dewey, 1899/1915.
43. "Pestalozzi's theory is rooted in 'universal educability' (Adelman, 2000, p. 106), a principle on which the common school movement is built. Pestalozzi's importance to the thinking of nineteenth-century, common-school reformers is argued by Barnard (1906) in *Pestalozzi and His Educational System*. Pestalozzi's focus on educating the poor altered how his contemporaries viewed educational access. Similarly, Dewey rose to prominence by being a champion of universal education. While his *School and Society* (1899/1915) does not explicitly address the topic of universal education, Dewey nevertheless creates a pedagogy rooted in the nature of children, in their interests and their inclinations. In this way Dewey, like Pestalozzi, helped establish a theoretical and practical basis for universal education" (Colvin and King, 2018, pp. 51–52).
44. On Pestalozzi, see Barlow, 1977; on Dewey's ideas, see Dewey, 1899/1915.
45. Dewey, 1978, p. 16.
46. I am referring here to Ortega's texts dated from 1906 till 1935, in particular: "La pedagogía del paisaje," in *El Imparcial* (Madrid), September 17 (1906); "La pedagogía social como problema político" (1910), *La hora del maestro* (1913); *La pedagogía de la contaminación* (1917); *Biología y Pedagogía*: "El Quijote en la escuela" (1920), "Pedagogía y anacronismo" (1923), *Elogio de las virtudes de la mocedad* (1925); *Para los niños españoles* (1928); *Misión de la Universidad* (1930), *En el centenario de una Universidad* (1931); "Sobre el estudiar y el estudiante," in La Nación (Buenos Aires), April 23; "Sobre las carreras," in La Nación (Buenos Aires), septiembre-octubre; "Prólogo" a: Pedagogía general derivada del fin de la educación, by F. J. Herbart (1935).

47. On Ortega's educational system, see García Morente, 1922; Maillo, 1955; Zaragüeta, 1955; Mantovani, 1962; Barrena Sánchez, 1971; Escolano, 1968; Morón Arroyo, 1968; McClintock, 1971; Vázquez Gómez, 1983; Bársena, 1983; Santolaria, 1983; Lledó, 1984; Rodríguez Huéscar, 1985; Gutiérrez Zuloaga, 1986; De Winter, 1992; Tabernero del Río, 1993, 2009; Alejos, 1999; Casado, 2001; Almeida Amoedo, 2002; Zamora Bonilla, 2004, 2024; Castelló Meliá, 2010; Botanch Callén, 2015; Valiente, 2016; Cabrero Blasco, 2017; De Haro Honrubia, 2020; Guo, 2020.
48. Hanuszkiewicz, 2019.
49. Natorp, 1912.
50. Natorp, 1974.
51. Natorp, 1909, 1920.
52. On Natorp's educational system, see by Natorp: Natorp, 1899, 1922; on Natorp: Jegelka, 1992; Lembeck, 1994; Matsuda and Hämäläinen, 2020.
53. On Hessen's educational system, see by Hessen: Hessen, 1923, 1924; 1930a, 1930b, 1938, 1939, 1968a, 1968b, 1997; on Hessen: Folkierska, 2005; Wieczorek, 2005.
54. Hanuszkiewicz, 2019.
55. Kramer, 1976; Murphy, 2006.
56. Standing, 1998; Murphy, 2006.
57. Murphy, 2006.
58. We would recommend to readers the 2010 edition of the work by Routledge.

## Bibliography

Aguilera Aguilera, C. (1965), "Pensamiento educacional de D. Miguel de Unamuno," *Calasencia* 11, 44, pp. 405–523.

Alejos, C. (1999), "La pedagogía social de Ortega y Gasset y su perspectiva actual," in J. Laspalas (coord.), *Historia y teoría de la educación. Estudios en honor del profesor Emilio Redondo García*, Pamplona: Eunsa, pp. 41–57.

Almeida Amoedo, M. I. (2002), *José Ortega y Gasset: A Aventura filosófica da educaçao*, Lisboa: Impresa Nacional-Casa da Moeda.

Barlow, T.A. (1997), *Pestalozzi and American Education*, Boulder, CO: Este Es.

Barnard, H. (1906), *Peztalozzi and his educational system*, Syracuse, NY: C. W. Bardeen.

Barrena Sánchez, J. (1971), "Los fines de la educación en José Ortega y Gasset," *Revista Española de Pedagogía*, 116, pp. 393–414.

Barros Dias, J. M. de (1994), "Miguel de Unamuno: a teorização da educação contra a modernidade da Pedagogia," *Broteria. Cultura e Informação* 139, 2–3, pp. 167–181.

Bársena, F. (1983), "La dimensión educativa del problema de la verdad en el pensamiento de José Ortega y Gasset," *Revista Española de Pedagogía*, 160, pp. 311–324.

Berdugo Gómez de la Torre, I. (2000), "Unamuno y la Universidad: rector e intelectual," in C. Flórez Miguel (coord.), *Tu mano es mi destino*, Salamanca: Ediciones Universidad de Salamanca, pp. 45–58.

Blanco Prieto, F. (2011), *Unamuno: professor y rector en la Universidad de Salamanca*, Salamanca: Hergar Ediciones Antema.

Blyth, A. (1981), "From individuality to character: The Herbartian sociology applied to education," *British Journal of Educational Studies*, XXIX (1), pp. 69–79.

Botanch Callén, J. L. (2015), "Elementos para una antropología filosófica de la educación en Ortega y Gasset," *Revista de Estudios Orteguianos*, 30, pp. 155–173.

Buonaventura Delgado, C. (1973), *Unamuno educador*, Madrid: Editorial Magisterio Español.

Cabrero Blasco, E. (2017), "El krausismo y la Institución Libre de Enseñanza en la filosofía de la educación de Ortega y Gasset. La vocación como prolegómeno para reformar la sociedad," *Ápeiron. Estudios de Filosofía*, 7, pp. 67–78.

Cadrecha Caparros, M. A. (1990), "John Dewey: propuesta de un modelo educativo: I. Fundamentos," *Aula Abierta*, 55, pp. 61–87.

Carreras Planas, C. (2015), "John Dewey i l'educaciy democratica," *Educaciy i Historia: Revista d'Histmria de l'Educaciy*, 25, pp. 21–42.

Casado, A. (2001), "Ortega y la educación: perfiles de una trayectoria," *Revista Española de Pedagogía*, LIX, 220, pp. 385–402.

Castelló Meliá, J. C. (2010), "Le experiencia de la lectura como pedagía de la vida en Ortega," *Revista de Estudios Orteguianos*, 220, pp. 385–402.

Catalán, M. (1991), "John Dewey: Los límites de la ética científica," *Agora*, 13/1, pp. 139–147.

Catalán, M. (2001), "Una presentación de John Dewey," *Daimon. Revista de Filosofía*, 22, pp. 127–134.

Cláudio Matos, J. (2011), "John Dewey e Aldous Huxley: o admirável e o impensável na formação social da mentalidade," *Conjectura Caxias do Sul* 16, 3, pp. 78–96.

Colvin, R. and King, Kelley M. (2018), "Dewey's educational heritage: the influence of Pestalozzi," *Journal of Philosophy & History of Education*, 68, 1, pp. 45–54.

De Garmo, C. (2001), *Herbart and Herbartians*, Honolulu: University Press of Pacific.

De Haro Honrubia, A. (2020), "Claves filosóficas de la pedagogía en la obra de Ortega," *Daimon. Revista Internacional de Filosofía*, 79, pp. 133–146.

De Winter, O. J. (1992), "Ortega y Gasset y el fin de la pedagogía," in C. Morón Arroyo (ed.), *Ortega y Gasset. Un humanista para nuestro tiempo*, Pennsilvania: Aldeeu Erie, pp. 69–84.

Dewey, J. (1899/1915), *The School and Society: Being three lectures*, Chicago, IL: The University of Chicago Press.

Dewey, J. (1916), "Education as necessity," in John Dewey, *Democracy and education. The middle works 1899–1924*, vol. 9, Carbondale: Southern Illinois University Press, pp. 4–13.

Dewey J. (1978), "The problem of truth," in John Dewey, *Democracy and education. The middle works 1899–1924*, vol. 9, Carbondale: Southern Illinois University Press, pp. 12–68.

Dewey, J. and Dewey, E. (1915/2016), *Schools of to-morrow*, Lago Vista TX: Grindl.

Dunken, H. B. (1969), *Herbart and education*, New York: Random House.

Escolano, A. (1968), "Los temas educativos en la obra de J. Ortega y Gasset," *Revista Española de Pedagogía*, 103, pp. 211–230.

Esteban, J. M. (2017), "John Dewey y la tragedia de los communes," *Éndoxa: Series Filosóficas*, 39, pp. 265–284.

Fenyő, I. (2016), "The reception of John Dewey in Hungary," *Espacio, Tiempo y Educación*, 3(2), pp. 183–205.

Fermoso Estébanez, P. (1991), "Bibliografía sobre John Dewey: Filosofía de la Educación," *Teoría de la educación*, 3, pp. 165–178.

Fernandes de Andrade, E. N. and Vinicius da Cunha, M. (2016), "A contribuição de John Dewey ao ensino da arte no Brasil," *Espacio, Tiempo y Educación*, 3(2), pp. 301–319.

Folkierska, A. (2005), *Sergius Hessen – pedagog odpowiedzialny*, Warszawa: Wydawnictwa Uniwersytetu Warszawskiego.

García Blanco, M. (1963),"Don Miguel y la Universidad," *Cuadernos de la Cátedra Miguel de Unamuno*, 13, pp. 13–32.

García Morente, M. (1922), "La pedagogía de Ortega y Gasset," *Revista de Pedagogía*, II-III, pp. 41–47, 95–101.

Gomes Ferreira, A., Mota, L., Cardoso Vilhena, C. (2019), "Discurso sobre a emergência da educação da infância formal em Portugal (1880–1950)," *História da Educação*, 23, pp. 1–33.

Gómez Molleda, M. (1963), "Unamuno y la polémica sobre la autonomía universitaria," *Cuadernos de la Cátedra Miguel de Unamuno*, 13, pp. 13–32.

Gómez Molleda, M. (1986), "Unamuno y la polémica sobre la autonomía universitaria," in *AA. VV. Perspectivas de España Contemporánea. Estudios en homenaje al professor V. Palacios Atard*, Madrid: Guthersa, pp. 355–399.

González Hernández, D. (2011), "El público y sus problemas. John Dewey en los estudios de comunicación," *Razón y Palabra*, 75, pp. 1–14.

Gordo Piñar, G. (2012), "El pensamiento educativo de Miguel de Unamuno," *Humanistyka i Przyrodoznawstwo*, 18, pp. 167–182.

Guo, Y. (2020), "El pensamiento pedagógico de José Ortega y Gasset y su proyecto educativo para España (1905–1938)," *Revista de Estudios Orteguianos*, 40, pp. 121–126.

Gutiérrez Zuloaga, I. (1986), "La pedagogía universitaria según Ortega y Gasset," in Gutiérrez Zuloaga, I. (ed.), *Homenaje a José Ortega y Gasset (1883–1983)*, Madrid: Universidad Complutense, pp. 23–42.

Hanuszkiewicz, W. (2019), "Concept of pedagogy as applied philosophy: Paul Natorp, John Dewey, and Sergius Hessen," *Argument: Biannual Philosophical Journal*, 9(2), pp. 201–223.

Hegel, G. F. (1991), *Elements of the philosophy of right*. Edited by Allen W. Wood. New York: Cambridge, 1991.

Herbart, J. F. (1982a), *Kleinere pädagogische Schnften*, Stuttgart.

Herbart, J. F. (1982b), *Pädagogische Grundschriften*, Stuttgart.

Herbart, J. F. (1982c), *Pädagogisch didaktische Schriften*, Stuttgart.

Herrero Castro, C. A. (1991), "Pensamiento social-educativo de Miguel de Unamuno: estructura y cambio social en la España del primer tercio del siglo XX," *Studia Paedagogia* 22, 22, pp. 55–79.

Hessen, S. (1923), *Osnovy pedagogiki. Vvedenie v prikladnuû filosofiû*, Berlin: Kn-vo Slovo.

Hessen, S. (1924), "Paul Natorp," *Russkaja Škola za Rubežom*, 2(10/11), pp. 1–8.

Hessen S. (1930a), "John Deweys Erziehungslehre," *Erziehung. Monatschrift für den Zusammenhang von Kultur end Erziehung in Wissenschaft und Leben*, 5, pp. 657–684.

Hessen, S. (1930b), "Der Zusammenbruch des Utopismus," in Boris Jakovenko (ed.), *Festschrift TH. G. Masaryk zum 80 Geburstage*, Bonn: Friedrich Cohen, pp. 107–120.

Hessen, S. (1938), *Szkoła i demokracja na przełome*, Warszawa: Nasza Księgarnia.

Hessen, S. (1939), *O sprcezcnościach i jedności wychowania. Zagadnienia pedagogikipersonalistycznej*, Lwów-Warszawa: Książnica-Atlas.

Hessen, S. (1968a), "Cnoty starożytne a cnoty ewangeliczne," in Sergius Hessen. *Studia z filosofii kultury* (A. Walicki, ed.), Warszawa: Państwowe Wydawnictwo Naukowe, pp. 194–268.

Hessen, S. (1968b), "Prawo i moralność," in Sergius Hessen *Studia z filozofii kultury* (A. Walicki, ed.),Warszawa: Państwowe Wydawnictwo Naukowe, pp. 269–313.

Hessen, S. (1997), "Pedagog," in Sergius Hessen, *Pisma pomniejsze* (W. Okón, ed.), Warszawa: Wydawnictwo "Zak," pp. 70–93.

Hilgenheger, N. (1993), "Johann Friedrich Herbart," *Prospects: the quarterly review of comparative education*, vol. XXIII, no. 3/4, pp. 649–644.

Horlacher, R. (2013a), "Do educational models impose standardization? Reading Peztalozzi historically," in Thomas Popkewitz (ed.), *Rethinking the history of education. Transnational perspectives on its questions, methods, and knowledge*, New York, NY: Palgrave Macmillan, pp. 135–156.

Horlacher, R. (2013b), "Schooling as a means of popular education. Peztalozzi's method as a popular education experiment," in Sjaak Braster (ed.), *A history of popular education: Educating the people of the world*, London, Routledge, pp. 65–75.

Horlacher, R. (2019), "Vocational and liberal education in Pestalozzi's educational theory," *Pedagogía y Saberes*, 50, pp. 109–120.

Jegelka, N. (1992), *Paul Natorp. Philosophie, Pädagogik, Politik*, Würzburg: Könighausen & Neumann.

Kant, I. (1960), *Religion within the limits of reason alone*. Part I. Translated by Theodore Greene and Hoyt Hudson. New York: Harper and Row Publishers, 1960.

Kant, I. (1996a), *Critique of practical reason*, in *The Cambridge edition of the works of Immanuel Kant: practical philosophy*. Translated by Mary J. Gregor. New York, NY: Cambridge University Press.

Kant, I. (1996b), *Metaphysics of Morals, in The Cambridge Edition of the Works of Immanuel Kant: practical philosophy*. Translated by Mary J. Gregor. New York, NY: Cambridge University Press.

Kant, I. (1996c), "What is enlightenment?," in *The Cambridge edition of the works of Immanuel Kant: practical philosophy*. Translated by Mary J. Gregor. New York, NY: Cambridge University Press.

Kant, I. (2001), *Groundwork for metaphysics of morals*. Edited by Allen W. Wood. New Haven, CN: Yale University Press.

Kant, I. (2007a), "Idea for a universal history with a cosmopolitan aim," in *The Cambridge edition of the works of Immanuel Kant: anthropology, history and education*. Translated by Allen Wood. New York, NY: Cambridge University Press.

Kant, I (2007b), "Lectures on pedagogy," in *The Cambridge edition of the works of Immanuel Kant: anthropology, history and education*. Translated by Robert B. Loudon. New York, NY: Cambridge University Press.

Kennedy, D. (2006), "John Dewey on children, childhood, and education," *Childhood & Philosophy* 2, 4, pp. 211–229.

Kramer, R. (1976), *Maria Montessori: a biography*, New York: G. P. Putnam's Sons.

Lembeck, K. H. (1994), *Platon in Marburg: Platon-Rezeption und Philosophiegeschichtsphilosophie bei Cohen und Natorp*, Würzburg: Könighausen & Neumann.

Lledó, E. (1984), La "Misión de la Universidad" de Ortega, entre las reformas alemanas y nuestra Universidad," *Sistema*, 59, pp. 7–18.

Luarsabishvili, V. (2019), "Miguel de Unamuno and John Dewey: the system of education and personal liberty," *Kultura i Wartości*, 28, pp. 277–291.

Madruga Méndez, J. (2005), *Miguel de Unamuno: profesor y político*, Salamanca: Gráficas Cervantes.

Maillo, A. (1955), "Las ideas pedagógicas de Ortega y Gasset," *Revista de Educación*, pp. 71–78.

Mann, H. (1846), "Ninth anual report of the secretary of the board of education," *The Common School Journal*, 8(13), pp. 193–208.

Mantovani, J. (1962), "La pedagogía de Ortega y Gasset," *Filósofos y educadores*, pp. 55–74.

Marías, J. (1953), *El existencialismo en España*, Bogota: Ediciones Universidad Nacional de Colombia.

Marías, J. (1967), *Miguel de Unamuno*, Madrid: Espasa-Calpe.

Matsuda, T. and Hämäläinen, J. (2020), "Launching Paul Natorp's *Sozialpädagogik* in Japan in the early twentieth century," *History of Education*, 50, 3, pp. 291–312.

McClintock, R. M. (1971), *Man and His Circumstances: Ortega as Educator*, New York: Columbia University Press.

Miovska-Spaseva, S. (2016), "The educational theory of John Dewey and its influence on educational policy and practice in Macedonia," *Espacio, Tiempo y Educación*, 3(2), pp. 207–224.

Morón Arroyo, C. (1968), *El sistema de Ortega y Gasset*, Madrid: Ediciones Alcalá.

Morón Arroyo, C. (2003), *Hacia el sistema de Unamuno: estudios sobre su pensamiento y creación literaria*, Palencia: Cálamo.

Múgica, L. R. (1909), *Más allá del Atlántico*, University of California Libraries.

Murphy, M. M. (2006), *The history and philosophy of education. Voices of educational pioneers*, Columbus: Pearson.

Natorp, P. (1899), *Sozialpädagogik: Theorie der Willenerziehung auf der Grundlage der Gemeinschaft*, Stuttgart: Fr. Frommans Verlag.

Natorp, P. (1909), *Peztalozzi. Sein Leben und seine Ideen*, Leipzig: Teubner.

Natorp, P. (1912), "Kant und die Marburger Schule," *Kant-Stuedien*, 17, pp. 193–221.

Natorp, P. (1920), *Der Idealismus Peztalozzis. Eine Neuuntersuchung der philosophischen Grundlagen seiner Erziehungslebre*, Leipzig: Felix Meiner.

Natorp, P. (1922), *Socialidealismus. Neue Richtlinien sozialer Erziehung*, Berlin: Springer.

Natorp, P. (1974), *Sozialpädagogik. Theorie der Willendbildung auf Grundlage der Gemeinschaft*, Paderborn: Schöningh.

Pallarès Piquer, M. and Muñoz Escalada, M. C. (2017), "La vigencia de Hannah Arendt y John Dewey en la acción docente del siglo XXI," *Foro de Educación*, 15(22), pp. 1–23.

Pestalozzi, J. H. (1801/1900), *How Gertrude teaches her children: an attempt to help mothers teach their own children and an account of the method: a report to the Society of Friends of Education, Burgordf*, Syracuse, NY: C. W. Bardeen.

Pestalozzi, J. H. (1801/1906), *Leonard and Gertrude*, Boston, MA: D. C. Health & Co.

Pestalozzi, J. H. (1998), "Die Methode," in Johann Heinrich Pestalozzi, *Sämtliche Werke*, Volume 13, Zurich: Neue Zürcher Zeitung, pp. 101–122.

Pettoello, R. (1988), *Introduzione a Herbart*, Roma: Bari.

Read, J. (2003), "Froebelian women: networking to promote professional status and educational change in the nineteenth century," *History of Education*, 32:1, pp. 17–33.

Rodríguez Huéscar, A. (1985), "Dimensiones de la acción educativa de Ortega," *Diálogos. Revista del Departamento de Filosofía de la Universidad de Puerto Rico*, año XX, pp. 121–139.

Rogacheva, Y. (2016), "The Reception of John Dewey's Democratic Concept of School in Different Countries of the World," *Espacio, Tiempo y Educación*, 3(2), pp. 65–87.

Rosales, J. M. (2012), "La retórica de la democracia y el liberalismo político en los escritos de John Dewey," *Revista de Estudios Políticos*, 155, pp. 185–206.

Rousseau, J.-J. (1987), *The basic political writings*, Indianapolis, IN: Hackett Publishing.

Rubin, R. M. (2010), "George Santayana and John Dewey Meet", *Limbo*, 30, pp. 31–52.

Rubio Latorre, R. (1974), *Educación y educador en el pensamiento de Unamuno*, Salamanca: Ediciones Instituto Pontífico San Pio X.

Santolaria, F. F. (1983), "Tres ensayos pedagógicos de Ortega," *Perspectivas pedagógicas*, 51, pp. 501–510.

Santos Gómez, M. (2011), "Limitaciones de la pedagogía de John Dewey," *Bordón*, 63, pp. 121–130.

Schmitz, J. N. (1964), *Herbart-Bibliographie (1842–1963)*, Weinheim: J. Beltz.

Skowroński, K. (2016), "Entre política y estética: la idea de la democracia liberal en la filosofía del arte de John Dewey," *La torre del Virrey. Revista de Estudios Culturales*, 19, 1, pp. 1–11.

Sotelino Losada, A. (2015), "A aprendizaxe-servizo en perspectiva. John Dewey como referente histórico," *Sarmiento*, 18–19, pp. 145–162.

Standing, E. M. (1998), *Maria Montessori, her life and work*, New York: Plume.

Tabernero del Río, S. (1993), *Filosofía y educación en Ortega y Gasset*, Salamanca: Editorial de la Universidad de Salamanca.

Tabernero del Río, S. (2009), "Libertad, razón y educación en J. Ortega y Gasset," *Foro de Educación*, 7, 11, pp. 85–101.

Taylor Xóchil, A. A. and Padilla, A. (2016), "John Dewey en México: Una experiencia compartida en el mundo rural," *Espacio, Tiempo y Educación*, 3(2), pp. 33–63.

Unamuno, M. de (1970), *Obras completas*, VIII, Madrid: Esceliser.

Unamuno, M. de (1973), "Mi religión," in Miguel de Unamuno, *Mi religión y otros ensayos breves*, Madrid: Espasa-Calpe.

Vaamonde Gamo, M. and Nubiola, J. (2016), "El legado feminista de John Dewey,"*Espacio, Tiempo y Educación*, 3(2), pp. 281–300.

Valkanova, Y. and Brehony, K. J. (2006), "The gifts and 'contributions': Friedrich Froebel and Russian education (1850–1929)," *History of Education*, 35:2, pp. 189–207.

Valiente, G. (2016), "La pedagogía social de Ortega y Gasset (1902–1914): una concepción comunitaria de la educación," *Tiempo y Sociedad*, 22, pp. 169–192.

Vázquez Gómez, G. (1983), "Perspectiva orteguiana de la pedagogía," *Teorema. Revista Internacional de Filosofía*, 13, 3/4, pp. 523–542.

Weston, P. (1998), *Friedrich Froebel. his life, times & significance*, London: Roehampton Institute.

Wieczorek, Z. (2005), *Filozofia wszechjedności Sergiusza Hessena*, Kraków: Wydawnictwa Uniwersytetu Jagiellońskiego.

Wolman, B. B. (1968), "The historical role of Johann Friedrich Herbart," in B. B. Wolman (ed.), *Historical roots of contemporary psychology*, New York: Harper & Row, pp. 29–46.

Zamora Bonilla, J. (2004), "El sentido humanista de la Universidad. Comentario a un texto de 1930: *Misión de la Universidad*, de José Ortega y Gasset," in Manuel Ángel Bermejo Castrillo (ed.), *Manuales y textos de enseñanza en la Universidad liberal. VII Congreso Internacional sobre la Historia de la Universidades Hispánicas*, Madrid: Instituto Antonio de Nebrija de la Universidad Carlos III, pp. 729–750.

Zamora Bonilla, J. (2024), "Unas notas sobre la pedagogía de Ortega y Gasset," *Daimon. Revista Internacional de Filosofía*, 91, pp. 7–21.

Zaragüeta, J. (1955), "El pensamiento pedagógico de José Ortega y Gasset," *Revista de Educación*, 38, pp. 65–70.

Zorić, V. (2016), "Influencia de John Dewey en las reformas educativas en Turquía y en la Unión soviética," *Espacio, Tiempo y Educación*, 3(2), pp. 101–130.

CHAPTER 2

# Education

## 2.1. Introduction

The Latin word "eductio" ("educatio") served to describe an action aimed at converting a lesser thing into a better one. Based on special techniques later defined as "pedagogy," the aim of instructing or educating an individual was the transformation of an ordinary person into a better creature with virtuous qualities. Thus, pedagogy as a science modifies the integral character of a person and attempts, on the one hand, to determine the form an educated individual may take and, on the other, to find the intellectual, moral, and aesthetic models necessary for the formation of an ideal person.[1]

Education was a widely discussed topic in Europe during the second half of the nineteenth and the beginning of the 20th century.[2] The crisis of ideas prominent in the second half of the 19th century,[3] the new views of the Romanticism theorists, and the unstable political situation in Europe before the First World War prepared the necessary environment for the development of new educational approaches. European countries engaged in activities to increase the level of general education among the population and to create a new life based on the modern challenges posed by complex historical and political realities. One such challenge was the defeat of German forces by Napoleon's army in 1806, during which the concept of *Bildung* aimed to find its way, as in the case of Germany, under the dominance of France and England.[4] Johann Gottlieb Fichte supported the idea of strengthening the educational platform and cultural purity. Fichte did not consider the teacher a mere transmitter of knowledge; rather, the teacher was seen as a storyteller on how to process the acquisition of knowledge and as an actor enacting this process. Fichte's ideas on state control of the university were not positively received by Schleiermacher and Humboldt. Schleiermacher insisted that the relation between state and university must not be direct: the state should protect university freedom, which would enable autonomous philosophical thinking and transform the university into an institution capable of developing traditions rather than abandoning them. Humboldt emphasized the importance of improving elementary schools and proposed a three-level system of education, which, together with Fichte and Schleiermacher's ideas, significantly influenced educational progress in Germany at the end of the 18th century.[5]

Education as a theoretical discipline has a rich history with clearly defined practical applications, making one very interesting observation detectable: that critical moments in its development were always conditioned by political, social, and humanitarian oscillations, as was the case with the defeat of German forces by Napoleon's army or during the Industrial Revolution in the 19th century, which resulted in multiple changes first in social and later in public health systems. The debate between two different approaches to education, or between *Bildung* and civic usefulness, which, for example, occurred in Germany almost three centuries ago, was rooted in the historical approach to the education system, dating back to Plato's aim to educate society first and individuals after,[6] and Seneca's demonstration of the necessity of the connection between school and life.[7] Passing through the ideas cultivated by Jean-Jacques Rousseau,[8] Immanuel Kant (his categorical imperative and moral imperative regarding how to treat people),[9] Johann Gottlieb Fichte (who considered it necessary to strengthen educational efforts),[10] Alexander von Humboldt (who proposed a system composed of elementary schools, secondary schools, and universities),[11] and Johann Heinrich Pestalozzi[12] (who laid a solid foundation for the connection of pedagogy and social well-being),[13] philosophers and educators in later generations, such as John Dewey,[14] Paul Natorp,[15] Miguel de Unamuno,[16] and José Ortega y Gasset,[17] to name a few, have formed their understanding of education in general, and of school and university education in particular.

The political and social crisis in 19th-century Spain, including the low level of literacy in the population,[18] not only conditioned the formation of intellectuals as a form of social response but also sparked a vivid polemic on the role of education in the creation and development of the nation. The Generation of 1898 played an important role in the development of modern Spanish society.[19] Among the main educators of society during this critical moment were Miguel de Unamuno and Ortega y Gasset.[20]

The awakening of national consciousness became visible in Japan since the 1980s,[21] aiming to build a Western-like civilization rooted in Japanese cultural traditions. This reformation was realized by the introduction of German *Sozialpädagogik*[22] and translation of special texts.[23]

From the second half of the nineteenth century, the development of educational thought became apparent in Russia. Liberal reforms that originated during the reign of Alexander II and succeeded in the development of a unified school system were continued by the efforts of Vasiliy Ivanovich Vodovosov, Grand Duchess Elena Pavlovna, Mikhail Borisovich Chistiakov, Lev Nikolaevich Tolstoy, Adelaida Semyonovna Simonovitch, Elizaveta Nikolaevna Vodovosova, and others.[24]

## 2.2. Ethics in Education

Why do ethics matter in education? Why should education be ethical, and how can ethics be used for educational purposes? Answers to these questions may define education as a social product that aims to share values related to social well-being and a happy life expectancy.[25]

Several factors may place ethics at the center of education. Political situation, cultural composition, philosophical constitution, and historical background of society are among them.

The place of ethics in education is determined, among other reasons, by the role of the latter in politics. Indeed, for centuries, especially during the building of nations and creation of nation-states, education, especially formal school education, was used as a tool for propagating the culture of majorities and for ignoring, and sometimes destroying, the culture of minorities. This was a form of state politics, forming the basis for monocultural education. Naturally, monocultural education was characterized by violence and destruction of cultures, as there may be few countries in the world where the population is composed of monoethnic groups of citizens. It became especially evident during the past century when international migration, facilitated by easy travel and conditioned by social, economic, and political difficulties, created additional obstacles for educational systems in immigrant countries. Less complicated were the cases when migrants entered new countries for a limited period of time and not on a permanent basis. Another, and totally different, situation was observed in the case of stable migration when people settled permanently without any concrete plans to leave the immigration country in the observable future. In this case, educational systems were conditioned to offer new approaches for the inclusion of migrants, especially their children, into the existing national educational curricula. These efforts were complicated from the 1970s when it became evident that migrants frequently wished to keep their culture, their language and refused to be assimilated. This was a reason that determined the necessity of the development of multicultural education, a new trend in modern educational systems that could facilitate the coexistence of people with different cultural backgrounds and, at the same time, help migrants' children to be included in a new and different society.[26]

Culture is another factor that determines the role of ethics in the development of society. *Multicultural* education, which semantically differs from *intercultural* education,[27] underlines the participation of different cultures in education. The role of this difference is so evident that a term like *antiracist education*, frequently used in the UK and Greece, was coined, as well as some other formulations, such as *education of minorities* or the *inclusion of diversity*. Distinct factors determined the necessity of considering cultural differences during education, such as acceptance of culture as an analytical category, the origin of different social movements in the United States, migration in Western European countries, understanding the role of culture as a marker of Europe's historical and cultural diversity, and the role of the international scientific community and supranational organizations in the formation of a scientific basis for the topic.[28] As a result, multicultural education found its place in contemporary educational systems, identifying necessities and approaches to a modern way of teaching.

Politics and culture are not the only reasons why ethics matter in education. Philosophy, or the way of accepting the surrounding world, is a domain of human activity supported by educational instruments. At distinct stages of the development of human society, positioning the self in the surrounding world was realized in different manners. This may be considered as the history of individualism, which can describe the possibilities of self-realization in different cultural epistemes and historical contexts. Starting from the feudal society, when the role of individuality in the development of society was almost non-observable, and passing through the Middle Ages, Renaissance, and Romanticism, individualism, as a human phenomenon, has played a decisive role in the transformation of mankind, being determined by the development of different spheres of human activity, such as political changes (the growing centralizing monarchism) and legal changes (the updating of Roman law of individualistic type from the twelfth century), the establishment of parliamentary systems (Medieval parliamentarism—from 1118 in Castile, from 1214 in England, and from the beginning of the XIV century in France), the birth of public opinion, the growth of monarchical absolutism from the end of the fifteenth century to the very moment of the French Revolution, the emergence and development of capitalism, the appearance of heresies, the progressive secularization of European society, the geographical discoveries of the fifteenth and sixteenth centuries, the birth of the progressive idea together with the crisis of authority and ideas regarding historical sense, nationalism, and the acceptance of people as entities with intellectual and political backgrounds, the French Revolution, technical and scientific development, the discovery of human-controlled energy capable of being used at any time and in any place, and social changes in the XIX century.[29]

History was, and continues to be, a domain that perhaps describes in a better way different activities realized by men in a fixed time context. The ways of accepting things and events in the form they exist, rejecting part of the historical past[30] and the development of social amnesia,[31] are conditioned by the indoctrination of generations that pass through educational systems. The composition of textbooks, including historical ones,[32] is based on the political benevolence of a nation to identify itself as a society with a vivid and rich past, traditions, and, what is most important, a historical perspective. Even though the expression "historical perspective" can sound like an oxymoron, many nations deeply believe in their historical mission, in their role in establishing and developing democratic societies, strengthening human rights, and drawing global human perspectives.

Recent publications indicate the role of ethics in teaching; among them are works by Felicity Haynes (arguing for an ethics of consequences, consistency, and care), Robert Nash (explanation of the necessity of certain rules, principles, and beliefs), Gert Biesta (going "beyond learning"), and Ken Strike (making links with John Rawls' social ethics).[33]

## 2.3. Education as a Value

Education is, and should be considered to be, a value. It is a value because it implies having the right to it, the right to be educated according to modern approaches and advances in education. As this right is universal, the different ways of its realization should be created and followed. As a value, education should be shared, forming an essential part of the development of modern human society.

At all stages of our intellectual development—be it preschool, school, college, or university education—society is the basic acting agent that determines the necessity and importance of providing educational facilities, such as printed and electronic study materials, the possibility of attending classes (including infrastructure, such as roads and school buses, etc., and technology, such as libraries and computer classes), and participating in teaching communication with peers and teachers. The next stage is the creation of modern possibilities for the exchange of schoolchildren and students, realized by different European and non-European programs that make international communication and familiarization with different cultural and historical epistemes possible. Spending part of the educational years at different universities opens new horizons and creates new perspectives for better human communication. One of the latest achievements of international university systems was the formation of CIVIS—European Civic University, founded by the alliance of eleven universities, including Aix-Marseille University, National and Kapodistrian University of Athens, University of Bucharest, The Université libre de Bruxelles, The Autonomous University of Madrid, Sapienza Università di Roma, Stockholm University, Eberhard Karls Universität Tübingen, University of Glasgow, Paris Lodron University of Salzburg, and University of Lausanne.[34]

In the complex world of modern human relations, education has found its way into health sciences. One of the basic approaches to building an educated, healthy, and civic society is the development of health education systems. Based on the publication of the Lalonde Report ("A New Perspective on the Health of Canadians")[35] and developed into the *Ottawa Charter for Health*, health education is defined as an activity that aims to achieve health or illness-related knowledge,[36] which has developed from an information-giving to an empowerment liberator approach. Health education has revived an interest in Freire's education paradigm, based on a three-stage methodological approach (listening, participatory approach, and action).[37]

## 2.4. Technologies in Education

Modern approaches to education could not be imagined without a prominent role played by technologies. Today, any visible and measurable advances in education are mostly due to the development of digital technologies, which represent a cornerstone for the development of novel teaching techniques. Technologies facilitate not only the building of the channel of communication between teachers and students but also create new possibilities for the improvement of interpersonal and international communication that develops educational traditions and creates a new paradigm for enhancing academic possibilities.

The idea of introducing novel methods of technological development into educational practice is not new. In the past century, an increased number of scientific publications were dedicated to the topic of the formation of a new epistemological basis for the development of scientific directions in education. Cultural studies, as well as its adjacent disciplines, such as studies of science, technologies, and societies, offered new insight into the development of modern educational systems,[38] connecting educational science with the formation of identity—individual[39] and collective identities[40]—in the framework of different cultural contexts.[41]

Digital processing systems stimulate active learning, involving students actively in the learning process, transforming them from passive listeners into actors who participate in the construction of knowledge and in the exploration of sources related to the understanding of new material. By playing a proper role in discovering and analyzing new material, students become more engaged in teaching and form a new reality that conditions the development of their academic imagination for deeper engagement in future professions. Bringing proper devices into the classroom, such as mobile phones that permit browsing the internet, creation of e-portfolios that allow the presentation of different materials in distinct formats, introducing flipped classrooms that permit discovering new content before classes start leading to a deeper understanding of the topic, sharing links of interest that form personal learning networks, or creating virtual learning environments that permit the flexibility of access to courses and their contents, help to modify standard schemes of education and make it more attractive and participatory for students of all specialties, fostering professional dialogue, and establishing emancipatory practices.[42]

In an article dedicated to the improvement of teaching via social science research, Gary King and Maya Sen indicate that rigorous education-related research is conducted, during the last years, in different fields of science, such as physics, chemistry, computer science, medicine, and nursing.[43] Even though research in education is characterized by certain difficulties attributed to the formation of reproducible research design (formation of experimental and control groups) or unique research tools (small unit of analysis or variables),[44] new approaches to education, especially the use of newer technologies, are widely observable.[45] The motivating role of social connections during both offline[46] and online[47] learning that conditions better understanding of study material after students discuss it with each other,[48] as well as the role of teaching for the formation of better teachers[49] and the importance of feedback for better learning outcomes,[50] will have an important impact on the elaboration of new teaching methods and on the development of new technological and innovational approaches.[51] Among the latter are online learning communities, which make possible the connection of learning with interpersonal relations,[52] thus creating a special place for the formation of new ideas with their successful application.[53] In this new and mutual ambiance, there is a special place for instructors, who can provide useful feedback to students, especially regarding the less clear questions and confusions which may be observable during learning.[54]

Another important innovation is online annotation systems, which permit the collaborative discussion of text and its annotation, resulting in better learning outcomes.[55] Among the modern interactive methods of learning are *peer-instruction*,[56] *open-source collaborative video technology*, created by Harvard University's Academic Technology Department's Collaborative Annotation Tool (CAT), letting students to hit "rewind" or stop the CAT playback and annotate the provided information, as well as improving the classroom experience;[57] *Perusall* (with the functions of annotating and highlighting the text, sectioning the class, avatars, upvoting, email notifications, assessment, and instructive tools); and *Email Lists* for enhancing social connections or computer-assisted peer instruction.

## Notes

1. Ortega y Gasset, 1983, pp. 508–509.
2. Boli et al., 1985; Soysal and Strang, 1989; Carl, 2009; Flecha García, 2011; Ballarino et al., 2013.
3. Fernández Sanz, 1997; Dip, 2002; Parcero, 2006.
4. Horlacher, 2019.
5. On Fichte, see Fichte, 1988, 2008; on Humboldt, see Humboldt, 2000; On Schleiermacher, see Schleiermacher, 2002, 2017.
6. Plato's Theory of Education. Edited by T. I. L. o. Philosophy. Vol. Vol VIII, Ancient Philosophy. London: Routledge.
7. Seneca, 2015.
8. Rousseau, 1979. On Rousseau, see Cranston, 1991, 1997; Iheoma, 1997; O'Hagan, 1999; Scholoz, 2001.
9. Hill, 1992.
10. *Reden an die deutsche Nation*, 1808.
11. *Der Königsberger und der Lithuanian Schulplan*, 1809.
12. By Pestalozzi, see Pestalozzi, 1801/1900, 1801/1906, 1951; on Pestalozzi, see Downs, 1975; Biber, 1994; Gutek, 1968.
13. Pestalozzi's ideas influenced the development of educational thought in different cultural epistemes, such as the Prussian school system (Johann Herbart and Friedrich Froebel), or American educational sphere (Horace Mann, Henry Barnard, Joseph Neef, and John Dewey). On this topic, see Froebel, 1826/2005; Barnard, 1906; Mann, 1846; Natorp, 1909; Lucas, 1977; Gutek, 1978; Colvin and King, 2018.
14. By Dewey, see Dewey, 1899/1915; Dewey and Dewey, 1915/2016; Dewey, 1938; on Dewey, see Cadrecha Caparros, 1990; Catalán, 1991, 2001; Kennedy, 2006; González, 2011; Santos Gómez, 2011; Rosales, 2012; Sotelino, 2015; Skowroński, 2016; Vaamonde Gamo and Nubiola, 2016; Esteban, 2017.
15. By Natorp, see Natorp, 1920, 1974, 2007; on Natorp, see Jegelka, 1992; Konrad, 2004; Henseler, 2012.
16. By Unamuno, see Unamuno, 1970a; Unamuno, 1970b; Unamuno, 1970c; on Unamuno, see Herrero Castro, 1991; Morón Arroyo, 2003; Gordo Piñar, 2012; Aguilera, 1965; Delgado Criado, 1973; Gómez Molleda, 1986; Rubio Latorre, 1974; Barros Dias, 1994; Blanco Prieto, 2011; García Blanco, 1963; Gómez de la Torre, 2000; Madruga Méndez, 2007.
17. McClintock, 1971; Zamora Bonilla, 2021.

18. As Felipe B. Pedraza Jiménez and Milagros Rodríguez Cáceres have noted, of the approximately 10 million that made up the Spanish population in 1800, only 6 percent, that is, about 600,000, could read; Pedraza Jiménez, Milagros Rodríguez Cáceres, 1982, p. 64.
19. An interesting volume was published by the Center of the edition of Spanish classics at the university of Valladolid: *Los textos del 98*, al cuidado de Juan Carlos Ara y José Carlos Mainer (Valladolid: Centro para la Edición de los Clásicos Españoles, MMII, 2002).
20. Unamuno, 1973, pp. 12–13.
21. Wilson, 2011.
22. Matsuda and Hämäläinen, 2020.
23. Waniek, 2018.
24. Valkanova and Brehony, 2006.
25. On the concept of *happiness*, see Brenan, 1973, pp. 58–80; Tatarkiewicz, 1976; Telfer, 1980; Grene, 1986, pp. 355–368; Sumner, 1999; Russell, 2006; McMahon, 2007; Dutt and Radcliff (eds.), 2009; Laycock, 2011; Zevnik, 2014; on *happiness* and *education*, see Noddings, 2003; on *happiness* and *universities*, see Gibbs, 2017.
26. Castles, 2009.
27. "Strictly speaking, a semantic distinction must be made between *multicultural* and *intercultural*. In multicultural education, the prefix *multi* describes the multiplicity of different cultures which live on the same territory and/or are taught in the same institution, for example in school or in higher education. In intercultural education the prefix *inter* underlines the interactive aspect. In most European countries, the scholarly discourse uses the term *intercultural education*, but in some countries, for example the United Kingdom and the Netherlands, *multicultural education* seems to be most frequent" (Allemann-Ghionda, 2009, p. 134).
28. Alleman-Ghionda, 2009.
29. Bousoño, 1981.
30. Oakeshott, 1983; White, 2014.
31. Blouin Jr. and Rosenberg, 2011, pp. 107–110.
32. Ingrao, 2009, 2010.
33. Gluchmanova, 2015.
34. The official webpage of CIVIS: <https://civis.eu/en>
35. Lalonde, 1974.

36. Tones, 1993.
37. Freire, 1972.
38. Trifonas and Jagger, 2018.
39. Turkle, 1994, 1997.
40. Gillespie, 1995; Lull, 1995; Casetti y Chio, 1999.
41. Rebollo Catalán, 2002.
42. Cambridge Assessment International Education. *Digital technologies in the classroom*. <https://www.cambridgeinternational.org/images/271191-digital-technologies-in-the-classroom.pdf>
43. King and Sen, 2013.
44. Chingos, 2013; King and Sen, 2013.
45. Mayer, 2003; Shea, 2006.
46. Summers and Svinicki, 2007.
47. Graff, 2003; Rovai, 2003.
48. Bonwell and Eison, 1991; Sorcinelli, 1991.
49. VanLehn et al., 2007.
50. Dubner and Levitt, 2006.
51. King and Sen, 2013.
52. Downes, 1999.
53. Crouch and Mazur, 2001.
54. Brown and Campione, 1996.
55. Hwang and Wang, 2004; Robert, 2009.
56. Mazur, 1997; Crouch and Mazur, 2001; Fagen et al., 2002.
57. King and Sen, 2013.
58. Miller et al., 2018.

# Bibliography

Allemann-Ghionda, C. (2009), "From intercultural education to the inclusion of diversity," in James A. Banks (ed.), *The Routledge international companion to multicultural education*, New York and London: Routledge, pp. 134–145.

Aguilera, C. (1965), "Pensamiento educacional de D. Miguel de Unamuno," *Calasencia* 11, 44, pp. 405–523.

Ballarino, G., Meschi, E. and F. Scervini (2013), "The expansion of education in Europe in the 20th Century," *AIAS*, GINI Discussion Paper 83.

Barnard, H. (1906), *Pestalozzi and his educational system*, Syracuse, NY: C. W. Bardeen.

Barros Dias, J. M. (1994), "Miguel de Unamuno: a teorização da educação contra a modernidade da Pedagogia," *Broteria. Cultura e Informação*, 139, 2-3, pp 167–181.

Biber, G. E. (1994), *Henry Pestalozzi and his plan of education*, Bristol: Themmes Press.

Blanco Prieto, F. (2011), *Unamuno: professor y rector en la Universidad de Salamanca*, Salamanca: Hergar Ediciones Antema.

Blouin Jr., F. X. and W. G. Rosenberg (2011), *Processing the past. Contesting authority in history and the archives*, New York: Oxford University Press.

Boli, J., Ramirez, F. and J. Meyer (1985), "Explaining the origins and expansion of mass education," *Comparative Education Review* 29, 2, pp. 145–170.

Bonwell, C. C., and Eison, J. A. (1991), *Active learning: creating excitement in the classroom. 1991 ASHE-ERIC higher education reports*, Washington, DC: ERIC Clearinghouse on Higher Education.

Bousoño, C. (1981), *Épocas literarias y evolución. Edad Media, Romanticismo, Época Contemporánea*, Madrid: Gredos.

Brenan, J. G. (1973), "Happiness, pleasure and utility," in Brenan, J., *Ethics and morals*, New York: Harper and Row.

Brown, A., and Campione, J. (1996), "Psychological theory and design of innovative learning environments: on procedures principles and systems," in Leona Schauble and Robert Glaser (eds.), *Innovations in learning: new environments for education*, Mahwah, NJ: Erlbaum, pp. 289–325.

Cadrecha Caparros, M. A. (1990), "John Dewey: propuesta de un modelo educativo: I. Fundamentos," *Aula Abierta*, 55, pp. 61–87.

Carl, J. (2009), "Industrialization and public education: social cohesion and social stratification," in Robert Cowen and Andreas M. Kazamias (eds.), *International handbook of comparative education. Springer international handbooks of education*, vol. 22, Dordrecht: Springer, pp. 503–518.

Casetti, F. and Chio, F. di (1999), *Análisis de la televisión. Instrumentos, métodos y prácticas de investigación*, Barcelona: Paidós.

Castles, S. (2009), "World population movements, diversity, and education," in James A. Banks (ed.), *The Routledge International Companion to Multicultural Education*, New York and London: Routledge, pp. 49–61.

Catalán, M. (1991), "John Dewey: Los límites de la ética científica," *Agora*, 13/1, pp. 139–147.

Catalán, M. (2001), "Una presentación de John Dewey," *Daimon. Revista de Filosofía*, 22, pp. 127–134.

Chingos, M. M. (2013), "Class size and student outcomes: research and policy implications," *Journal of Policy Analysis and Management*, 32 (2), pp. 911–938.

Colvin, R. and K. M. King (2018), "Dewey's educational heritage: the influence of Pestalozzi," *Journal of Philosophy & History of Education*, vol. 68, 1, pp. 45–54.

Cranston, M. (1991), *Jean-Jacques: the early life and work of Jean-Jacques Rousseau 1712–1754*, Chicago: The University of Chicago Press.

Cranston, M. (1997), *The solitary self: Jean-Jacques Rousseau in exile and adversity*, 3 vols., London: Allen Lane.

Crouch, C. H. and Mazur, E. (2001), "Peer instruction: ten years of experience and results," *American Journal of Physics*, 69, p. 970.

Delgado Criado, B. (1973), *Unamuno educador*, Madrid: Editorial Magisterio Español.

Dewey, J. (1899/1915), *The school and society: being three lectures*, Chicago, IL: The University of Chicago Press.

Dewey, J. (1938), *Experience and education*, New York, NY: Simon & Schuster.

Dewey, J. and Dewey, E. (1915/2016), *Schools of to-morrow*, Lago Vista TX: Grindl.

Dip, P. C. (2002), "La crisis de los valores cristianos en el siglo XIX: Kierkegaard y Nietzsche," *Universitas Philosophica*, 38, pp. 191–204.

Downes, S. (1999), *Creating an online learning community (PowerPoint slides)*, Edmonton: VIRTUAL School Symposium.

Downs, R. (1975), *Heinrich Pestalozzi: father of modern pedagogy*, Boston: Twayne Publishers.

Dubner, S. J. and Levitt, S. D. (2006), "Freakonomics: a star is made," *New York Times Magazine*, May 7.

Dutt, A. and Radcliff, B. (eds.) (2009), *Happiness, economics and politics*, Cheltenham: Edward Elgar.

Esteban, J. M. (2017), "John Dewey y la tragedia de los communes," *Éndoxa*, 39, pp. 265–284.

Fagen, Adam P., Crouch, C. H. and Mazur, E. (2002), "Peer instruction: results from a range of classrooms," *Physics Teacher*, 40 (1), pp. 206–209.

Fernández Sanz, A. (1997), "El problema de España entre dos siglos (XIX–XX)," *Anales del Seminario de Historia de la Filosofía*, 14, pp. 203–222.

Fichte, J. G. (1988), *Early philosophical writings*, Ithaca and London: Cornell University Press.

Fichte, J. G. (2008), *Addresses to the German nation*, Cambridge, UK: Cambridge University Press.

Flecha García, C. (2011), "Education in Spain: close-up of its history in the 20th century," *Analytical Reports in International Education* 4, 1, pp. 17–42.

Freire, P. (1972), *Teoría y práctica de la liberación*, Madrid: Marsiega.

Froebel, F. (1826/2005), *The education of man*, Mineola, NY: Dover.

García Blanco, M. (1963), "Don Miguel y la Universidad," *Cuadernos de la Cátedra Miguel de Unamuno*, 13 pp. 13–32.

Gibbs, P. (2017), *Why universities should seek happiness and contentment?*, London: Bloomsbury.

Gillespie, M. (1995), *Television, ethnicity and cultural change*, London: Routledge.

Gluchmanova, M. (2015), "The importance of ethics in the teaching profession," *Procedia – Social and behavioral Sciences*, 176, pp. 509–513.

Gómez Molleda, M. (1986), "Unamuno y la polémica sobre la autonomía universitaria," *Cuadernos de la Cátedra Miguel de Unamuno*, 13, pp. 13–32.

Gómez de la Torre, I. B. (2000), "Unamuno y la Universidad: rector e intelectual," in Flórez Miguel, C. (coord.), *Tu mano es mi destino*, Salamanca: Ediciones Universidad de Salamanca, pp. 47–58.

González, D. (2011), "El público y sus problemas. John Dewey en los estudios de comunicación," *Razón y Palabra*, 75, pp. 1–14.

Gordo Piñar, G. (2012), "El pensamiento educativo de Miguel de Unamuno," *Humanistyka i Przyrodoznawstwo*, 18, pp. 167–182.

Graff, M. (2003), "Individual differences in sense of classroom community in a blended learning environment," *Journal of Educational Media*, 28 (2–3), pp. 203–210.

Grene, M. (1986), "In and on friendship," in Alan Donagan, Anthony N. Perovich, Jr. and Michael V. Wedin (eds.), *Human nature and natural knowledge. essays presented to Marjorie Grene on the occasion of her seventy-fifth birthday*, Dordrecht: D. Reidel Publishing Company pp. 355–368.

Gutek, G. (1968), *Pestalozzi and education*, Prospect Heights, IL: Waveland Press.

Gutek, G. (1978), *Joseph Neef: The Americanization of Pestallozianism*, Tuscaloosa: University of Alabama Press.

Henseler, J. (2012), "Paul Natorp (1854–1924)," in Bernd Dollinger (ed.), *Klassiker der Pädagogik*, Wiesbaden: VS Verlag für Sozialwissenschaften, pp. 179–198.

Herrero Castro, C. A. (1991), "Pensamiento social-educativo de Miguel de Unamuno: estructura y cambio social en la España del primer tercio del siglo XX," *Studia Paedagogia*, 22, 22, pp. 55–79.

Hill, T. (1992), *Dignity and practical reason in Kant's moral theory*, Ithaca: Cornell University Press.

Horlacher, R. (2019), "Vocational and Liberal Education in Pestalozzi's Educational Theory", *Pedagogía y Saberes*, 50, pp. 109–120.

Humboldt, W. (2000), "Theory of Bildung," in Ian Westbury, Stefan Hopmann & Kurt Riquarts (eds.), *Teaching as a reflective practice. The German Didactik tradition*, Mahwah, NJ: Lawrence Erlbaum Associates, pp. 57–61.

Hwang, W. Y. and Wang, C. Y. (2004), "A study on application of annotation system in web-based materials," in *Proceedings of GCCE' 04: the 8th Global Chinese Conference on Computers in Education*. Hong Kong, China.

Iheoma, E. (1997), "Rosseau's views on Teaching," *Journal of Educational Thought*, 31, pp. 69–81.

Ingrao, C. (2009), "Weapons of mass instruction: schoolbooks and democratization in Central Europe," *Journal of Educational Media, Memory, and Society*, 1, 1, pp. 180–189.

Ingrao, C. (2010), "Western intervention in Bosnia: operation deliberate force," in Bruce A. Elleman and Sarah C. M. Paine (ed.), *Naval coalition warfare: from the Napoleonic Wars to Operation Iraqi Freedom*, London: Routledge, pp. 169–182.

Jegelka, N. (1992), *Paul Natorp. Philosophie, Pädagogik, Politik*, Würzburg: Könighausen & Neumann.

Kennedy, D. (2006), "John Dewey on children, childhood, and education," *Childhood & Philosophy*, 2, 4, pp. 211–229.

King, G. and Sen, M. (2013), "How social science research can improve teaching," *The Teacher*, July, pp. 621–629.

Konrad, F.-M. (2004), "Sozialpädagogik und Volksschulreform. Paul Natorp in den schulpolitischen Kämpfen seiner Zeit," *Zeitschrift für Sozialpädagogik*, 2, pp. 338–360.

Lalonde M. (1974), "A new perspective on the health of Canadians", *Vasa*, 32(6), p. 76.

Laycock, R. (2011), *Happiness: lessons from a new science*, London: Penguin.

Lucas, C. J. (1977), *Teacher education in America*, New York, NY: St. Martin's.

Lull, J. (1995), *Media, communications, culture. A global approach*, Cambridge: Polity Press.

Madruga Méndez, J. (2007), *Miguel de Unamuno: profesor y político*, Salamanca: Gráficas Cervantes.

Mann, H. (1846), "Ninth annual report of the secretary of the board of education," *The Common School Journal*, 8 (13), pp. 193–208.

Matsuda, T. and Hämäläinen, J. (2020), "Launching Paul Natorp's *Sozialpädagogik* in Japan in the early twentieth century," *History of Education*, 50, 3, pp. 291–312.

Mayer, R. E. (2003), "The promise of multimedia learning: using the same instructional design methods across different media," *Learning and Instruction*, 13 (2), pp. 125–139.

Mazur, E. (1997), *Peer instruction: a user's manual*, Upper Saddle River, N. J.: Prentice Hall.

McClintock, R. (1971), *Man and his circumstances: Ortega as educator*, New York: Teachers College Press.

McMahon, D. (2007), *The pursuit of happiness*, London: Penguin.

Miller, K., Lukoff, B., King, G. and Mazur, E. (2018), "Use of a social annotation platform for pre-class reading assignments in a flipped introductory physics class," *Front. Educ.*, 3 (8).

Morón Arroyo, C. (2003), *Hacia el sistema de Unamuno: estudios sobre su pensamiento y creación literaria*, Plasencia: Calamo.

Natorp, P. (1909), *Pestalozzi. Sein Leben und seine Ideen*, Leipzig: Teubner.

Natorp, P. (1920), *Sozial-Idealismus: Neus Richtlinien Sozialer Erziehung*, Berlin: Verlag von Julius Springer.

Natorp, P. (1974), *Sozialpädagogik. Theorie der Willendbildung auf Grundlage der Gemeinschaft*, Paderborn: Schöningh.

Natorp, P. (2007), *Religion innerhalb der Grenzen der Humanität – ein Kapitel zur Grundlegung der Sozialpädagogik*, Saarbrücken: VdM Verlag Dr. Müller.

Noddings, N. (2003), *Happiness and education*, Cambridge: Cambridge University Press.

Oakeshott, M. (1983), *On history and other essays*, Oxford: Basil Blackwell.

O'Hagan, T. (1999), *Rousseau*, New York: Routledge.

Ortega y Gasset, J. (1983), "Educación," in José Ortega y Gasset, *Obras Completas*, I, Madrid: Alianza, pp. 508–509.

Parcero, J. A. (2006), "La crisis de la fundamentación de los derechos humanos en el siglo XIX," in Margarita Moreno-Bonett, María Del Refugio González Domínguez (coords.), *La génesis de los derechos humanos en México*, México: Universidad Nacional Autónoma de México, pp. 219–228.

Pedraza Jiménez, F. B., Rodríguez Cáceres, M. (1982), *Manual de literatura española. VI. Época romántica*, Pamplona: Cénlit Ediciones.

Pestalozzi, J. H. (1801/1900), *How Gertrude teaches her children: An attempt to help mothers teach their own children and an account of the method: A report to the Society of Friends of Education*. 2nd edition. Syracuse, NY: C. W. Bardeen.

Pestalozzi, J. H. (1801/1906), *Leonard and Gertrude*, Boston, MA: D. C. Health & Co.

Pestalozzi, J. H. (1951), *The education of a man: Aphorisms*, New York, NY: Philosophical Library. Rosales, J. M. (2012), "La retórica de la democracia y el liberalismo político en los escritos de John Dewey," *Revista de Estudios Políticos*, 155, pp. 185–206.

Rebollo Catalán, Mª A. (2002), "La investigación educativa sobre nuevas tecnologías: una aproximación sociocultural", *Enseñanza*, 20, pp. 113–126.

Robert, C. A. (2009), "Annotation for knowledge sharing in a collaborative environment", *J. Knowl. Manag.*, 13, pp. 111–119.

Rosales, J. M. (2012), "La retórica de la democracia y el liberalismo político en los escritos de John Dewey", *Revista de Estudios Políticos*, 155, pp. 185–206.

Rousseau, J.-J. (1979), *Emile, or on education*, New York: Basic Books.

Rovai, A. P. (2003), "The relationships of communicator style, personality-based learning style, and classroom community among online graduate students," *The Internet and Higher Education*, 6(4), pp. 347–363.

Rubio Latorre, R. (1974), *Educación y educador en el pensamiento de Unamuno*, Salamanca: Ediciones Instituto Pontífico San Pio X.

Russell, B. (2006), *The conquest of happiness*, London: Routledge Classics.

Santos Gómez, M. (2011), "Limitaciones de la pedagogía de John Dewey," *Bordón*, 63 (3), pp. 121–130.

Schleiermacher, F. (2002), *Lectures on philosophical ethics*, Cambridge: Cambridge University Press.

Schleiermacher, F. (2017), "Occasional thoughts on German universities in the German sense," in Louis Menand, Paul Reitter, and Chad Wellmon (eds.), *The rise of the research university: a sourcebook*, Chicago: University of Chicago Press, pp. 45–66.

Scholoz, S. (2001), *On Rousseau*, Belmont, CA: Wadsworth/Thomson Learning.

Seneca, L. A. (2015), *Letters on ethics to Lucilius*, Chicago, IL: The University of Chicago Press.

Shea, P. (2006), "A study of students' sense of learning community in online environments," *Journal of Asynchronous Learning Networks*, 10 (1), pp. 35–44.

Skowroński, K. (2016), "Entre política y estética: la idea de la democracia liberal en la filosofía del arte de John Dewey," *La torre del Virrey. Revista de Estudios Culturales*, 19, 1, pp. 1–11.

Sorcinelli, M. D. (1991), "Research findings on the seven principles," *New Directions for Teaching and Learning*, 47, pp. 13–25.

Sotelino, A., (2015), "A aprendizaxe-servizo en perspectiva. John Dewey como referente histórico," *Sarmiento. Revista Galego-Portuguesa de Historia da Educación*, 18–19, pp. 145–162.

Soysal, N. Y. and D. Strang (1989), "Construction of the first mass education systems in nineteenth-century Europe," *Sociology of Education* 62, 4, pp. 277–288.

Summers, J. J. and Svinicki, M. D. (2007), "Investigating classroom community in higher education," *Learning and Individual Differences*, 17(1), pp. 55–67.

Sumner, L. W. (1999), *Welfare, happiness and ethics*, Oxford: Clarendon Press.

Tatarkiewicz, W. (1976), *Analysis of happiness*, Hague: Martinus Nijhoff.

Telfer, E. (1980), *Happiness*, London: Macmillan.

Tones, K. (1993), "Changing theory and practice: Trends in methods, strategies and settings in health education", *Health Education Journal*, 52(3), pp. 125–139. https://doi.org/10.1177/001789699305200305

Trifonas, P. P. and Jagger, S. (2018), *Handbook of cultural studies and education*, Abingdon: Routledge.

Turkle, S. (1994), "Constructions and reconstructions of self in virtual reality: playing in the MUDs," *Mind, Culture and Activity*, 1:3, pp. 158–167.

Turkle, S. (1997), *Life on the screen: Identity in the age of internet*, New York: Touchstone.

Unamuno, M. de (1970a), "De la enseñanza superior en España," in Miguel de Unamuno, *Obras completas*, vol. III, Madrid: Esceliser.

Unamuno, M. de (1970b), "Discurso de Orense," in Miguel de Unamuno, *Obras completas*, vol. VII, Madrid: Esceliser.

Unamuno, M. de (1970c), "La enseñanza universitaria," in Miguel de Unamuno, *Obras completas*, vol. VII, Madrid: Esceliser.

Unamuno, M. de (1973), "Mi religión," in Miguel de Unamuno, *Mi religión y otros ensayos breves*, Madrid: Espasa-Calpe, pp. 9–15.

Vaamonde Gamo, M. and Nubiola, J. (2016), "El legado feminista de John Dewey," *Espacio, Tiempo y Educación*, 3(2), pp. 281–300.

Valkanova, Y. and Brehony, K. J. (2006), "The gifts and 'contributors': Friedrich Froebel and Russian education (1850–1929)," *History of Education*, 35, 2, pp. 189–207.

VanLehn, K., Graesser, A. C., Jackson, G. T., Jordan, P., Olney, A., & Rose, C. P. (2007), "When are tutorial dialogues more effective than reading?", *Cognitive Science*, 31, pp. 3–62.

Waniek, I. (2018), "Translation as a way of educating the nation: the case of Meiji Japan," *Euromentor Journal*, 3, pp. 55–67.

White, H. (2014), *The practical past*, Evanston, IL: Northwestern University Press.

Wilson, S. (2011), "The discourse of national greatness in Japan (1890–1919)," *Japanese Studies*, 1, pp. 35–51.

Zamora Bonilla, J. (2021), "El impacto de Ortega. La percepción de sus discípulos y colaboradores," *Anales del Seminario de Historia de la Filosofía*, 38 (3), pp. 217–513.

Zevnik, L. (2014), *Critical perspectives in happiness research*, Dordrecht: Springer.

CHAPTER 3

# Research

## 3.1. Introduction

Referring to the words of Professor Wiggers, Bernardo A. Houssay noted that the English word "research" is more expressive compared to the Spanish "investigación." It signifies looking again and again, re-examining with new and better methods, and discovering new things.[1] Research is considered an attempt to derive new knowledge that can be generalized, answering questions using rigorous methods of investigation, and generating and testing hypotheses.[2]

Higher education consists of two main components: teaching and research. The Bologna Process (1999), Berlin Communiqué (2003), and London Communiqué (2007), among other significant documents, acknowledge the role of knowledge in social and human growth. This includes the necessity of economic development for social cohesion, based on individual contributions from society members. Universities play an important role in this framework, connecting professional studies with everyday life. Teaching and research are based on contemporary social, political, economic, and demographic matters, as well as other public health components that determine human development within a specific time context. Social values are formed inside universities and disseminated outside to different societal layers, contributing to the continuous education of its members and the prevention of diseases. Thus, universities are crucial for building a healthy society, facilitating the development of healthcare systems, and implementing public health projects. From this point forward, universities acquire a function of social responsibility, based on ethical and community principles, resulting in the formation of responsible and tolerant citizens.[3]

In an article discussing the role of science, knowledge, and society in university research, Armando Alcántara Santuario reviews the university as the home of science.[4] Based on the works of Daniel Wolfe, Burton Clark, Simon Schwartzman, Teresa Pacheco, and Philip Altbach, the researcher describes the history of universities hosting science in various countries, including the United States, UK, and Germany, from the late 19th century.[5] He also discusses the different historical experiences of establishing research centers inside or outside universities, as seen in the Soviet Union.[6] In parallel with these reforms, 50 major universities in the United States were labeled as "research universities," where scientific investigation became a primary focus. Another interesting historical example is the Latin American universities, which provide a high level of autonomy, independence, and mobility for research staff. The situation in newly industrialized countries like Malaysia, Singapore, South Korea, and Taiwan is impressive, demonstrating modern scientific infrastructure at universities.

Different approaches to positioning science within or outside the higher education system were preceded by critical revisions of the nature of science and the mission of universities. Various authors, educators, philosophers, and public figures have discussed the roles of both science and universities in creating values in modern society. American philosopher and educational reformer John Dewey revised the education system's different levels, paying special attention to the nature of science. According to Dewey, science is knowledge derived from observation, reflection, and testing, "deliberately adopted to secure a settled, assured subject matter."[7] Science revises current understandings and knowledge, highlighting what is mistaken. It represents a form of knowledge that controls activities producing environmental changes, thus representing the final stage of knowledge.

Michael Oakeshott, a professor of political science at Cambridge University and the London School of Economics, considered the university to be "a manner of human activity," not a machine seeking to achieve or produce something. Oakeshott described the university as a place where all the necessities for the pursuit of learning are gathered to establish a conversation and impart the manners of that conversation.[8]

The distinction drawn by Oakeshott between the "pursuit of learning" and the "acquisition of knowledge" aligns with Jürgen Habermas's understanding of the university's role. It does not limit itself to "mere academic career preparations" and the "acquisition of expert knowledge." Rather, it introduces students to scientific thinking, "offering informed interpretations and diagnoses of contemporary events, and by taking concrete political stands."[9]

The topic of science as part of the university system has also been analyzed outside of the mentioned cultural contexts, with Spanish and Russian experiences being particularly interesting. Notably, two famous scientists from these countries, José Ortega y Gasset[10] and Vladimir Vernadsky,[11] expressed almost identical ideas about the mission of the university. Although Ortega represented the humanities and Vernadsky the natural sciences, both viewed universities as primary research centers.

Over time, Spain has developed a high level of university research;[12] scientific work in Russia has been conducted in research institutions outside universities, as part of the Soviet Academy of Sciences. However, the initial reception of science as an integral part of university life was similar in both countries.

The role of scientific research at universities has increased over time. The *Carnegie Classification of Institutions of Higher Learning*[13] distinguishes between *Research Universities* and *Teaching Colleges*. Research fosters the coexistence of different economic, technical, ideological, and cultural perspectives within the university, influencing the desired use and interpretation of accumulated research data. Independent research is combined with accepted values, forming the political and ideological narrative of specific societies. Thus, research is a crucial tool for understanding national reality and detecting governmental and professional interests, such as the creation of the *National Endowment for the Humanities*, *National Endowment for the Arts*, and *National Science Foundation*.

## 3.2. Ethics in Research

Why does ethics matter in research? Why should research be ethical, and how can ethics contribute to research rigor? Answers to these questions position research at the center of modern human activity.

From a philosophical perspective, research is as ethically valid as education. The same factors important for ethical education—political orientation, cultural composition, philosophical constitution, and historical background—also apply to ethical research.

Politics became interested in research soon after the French Revolution when it became clear that researchers could provide an evidence-based basis for political solutions. Since then, researchers have been invited and financed by states and governments, facilitating scientific investigations and increasing bias in research. Financing is always in the interests of the donors, making researchers dependent on the sources of investment. This is observable not only in biomedical sciences, where expensive laboratories need modern equipment, but also in social sciences, where political discourse benefits from philosophical, psychological, economic, historical, educational, and linguistic investigations financed by state scientific agencies or private foundations associated with political power. This context necessitates an ethical perspective in scientific investigation.

In the context of international collaboration, research today is inherently transdisciplinary and multicultural. The notion of *transdisciplinarity*, used to describe scientific research practice and science policy, is considered a development of the earlier concept of *interdisciplinarity*. While *interdisciplinarity* refers to "concrete cooperation with a finite duration," *transdisciplinarity* implies "enduring and systematic cooperation" that changes subject matter and disciplines. It represents scientific work addressing non-scientific problems, such as environmental, energy, and healthcare policy issues, as well as an intrascientific principle concerning scientific knowledge and research.

Joint publications are more productive and prestigious, and publishing in international houses ensures wide diffusion and high citation numbers. Special lists of editorials indicate the expertise of publishing houses in specific sciences.[14] Some other questions regarding publication are how to select publishing houses for concrete manuscript, as there are many, and how to define a general strategy for publishing—some researchers prefer to publish in a single publishing house, others are constantly looking for new contacts and possibilities. Ethical rules should be followed to avoid disrespect and non-collegial treatment when selecting publishing houses and defining publishing strategies.

The philosophy of research involves understanding the reasons and mechanisms for conducting social and biomedical research. Research mechanisms, including methodological instruments and data interpretation, distinguish different sciences and indicate their role in societal development. Research aims to improve life quality and increase life expectancy. Society should benefit from research equally, and these benefits should be immediate, making life easier, happier, and more acceptable.

The history of research provides a panoramic view of its development over past centuries, describing research's role in manipulating societies (connecting research with politics),[15] its role in cultural development (connecting research with culture),[16] and its role in nation formation (connecting research with philosophy).[17-18]

Ethical approaches in research cover internal (within the research community) and external (social responsibility) ethical norms, defining specific forms of scientific conduct and misconduct. Researchers have obligations to patients/volunteers in clinical trials and to experimental animals. Ethical values are universal and absolute; research should benefit all members of society equally, regardless of their characteristics (ethnic pertinence, political views, financial possibilities, etc.). Different ethical frameworks and theories are formed and criticized, complicating universal agreement on key ethical approaches to research. Based on what is estimated as being ethical or non-ethical—righteous act, act's good consequences, or the person that performs an act—different ethical frameworks and theories are formed and formulated, all of them being subjected to certain criticism that complicates the universal agreement on the key moments of ethical approaches to research.[19]

Nicholas Walliman summarizes two aspects of ethical issues in research: a) the researcher's individual values related to honesty, frankness, and personal integrity, and b) the researcher's treatment of participants, including informed consent, confidentiality, anonymity, and courtesy.[20]

Ethical issues arise at each stage of research, including the nature of the project, its context, procedures, data collection methods, and data dissemination.[21]

The notions of "scientific conduct" and "scientific misconduct" describe correct and incorrect activities. Merton, Tranøy, and others discuss basic norms necessary for scientific work.[22] Chubin identified seven causes of research misconduct: psychopathy, unbridled ambition, pressure for publication, competition for federal support, the "lab-chief" system, peer-review system failures, and lack of replication and sloppiness.[23]

Research fraud aims to generate false data intentionally, with fabrication, falsification, and plagiarism being the most common types. Researchers' subjective interests may lead to relevant results being omitted during publication. Misconduct can also arise from ignorance of accepted scientific standards, granted authorship, or failing to disclose conflicts of interest.[24]

The complex nature of ethical norms and diverse views on ethics have led to mechanisms regulating research ethics, such as ethics committees and ethical codes. The codes are formulated by professional societies, committees and associations—such as British Educational Research Association (<http://www.bera.ac.uk>), British Psychological Society (<http://www.bps.org.uk>), British Sociological Association (<http://www.britsoc.co.uk>), Danish Committees on Scientific Dishonesty, American Educational Research Association (<http://www.aera.net>), American Psychological Association's *Ethical Principles and Code of Conduct* (<http://www.apa.org>), American Sociological Association (<http://www.asanet.org>), World Medical Association Declaration of Helsinki: *Ethical Principles for Medical Research Involving Human Subjects*, Oviedo Convention, and many others.

## 3.3. Research as Value

Research is one of the main values of modern university life. As Bill Readings has noted, the university becomes modern when it is responsible for the relation between the subject and the state, based on its dual mission of teaching and research.[25] Carrying the function of producing and disseminating knowledge, research becomes an important tool for professional self-expression. Different branches of science, especially biomedical sciences, are wholly based on the accumulation of new research data. It is acknowledged that: "Evidence-Based Medicine (or health care) sees clinical expertise as the ability to integrate patient circumstances, research evidence, and patient preferences to help patients arrive at optimal diagnostic and treatment decisions."[26] The idea of science is a constant reinvention of itself, thriving on the mortality of knowledge that results in rediscovering itself.[27]

Seeking universal truth is a profession; researchers are committed to it.[28] The composition of our universe, our place in it, and the function we fulfill have been topics of inquiry across generations. Summarizing the historical experience of discovering the truth, we find three basic operations or intentions: *experience, reasoning,* and *research*. Research can be seen as part of the first two: *reasoning*, as it uses its methods, and *experience*, as it relies on concrete techniques and procedures that permit testing hypotheses and drawing conclusions.[29]

From these basic approaches, *research* possesses three main distinguishing characteristics: 1) systematic and controlled nature, 2) empirical essence, and 3) self-correcting nature. The first characteristic is based on the *inductive-deductive* method, considered a two-phase activity: 1) accumulating empirical data to build theoretical generalizations (*induction*), and 2) extending these generalizations to all relevant reality (*deduction*). This is the *hypothetico-deductive* method, which combines *induction* and *deduction* to identify problems, develop hypotheses based on observations, chart their implications by deduction, and test the hypotheses to accept or reject them. Scientific research methods can be roughly divided into *inductive-deductive* (or *empirical*) and *theoretical*, the latter aiming to construct a scientific theory based on *axioms* (hence the name *axiomatic method*), which leads to theorems through logical proof.

*Observation* is a critical stage for formulating conclusions: while deduction entails inference from *axioms* (or general statements) to specific statements via logic, and *induction* entails inference from particular statements to general ones, *observation* helps form a hypothesis for deduction, called the best explanation or *abduction*. Research or the scientific approach to reality also involves observation: researchers formulate hypotheses, test them, obtain data, and disseminate results. At the same time, *observation* may also involve personal experience, known as *lay* knowledge, formed from lived and felt experiences and deduced without critical assessment.[30]

## 3.4. Technologies in Research

Modern life is inseparable from scientific development, which influences planning and conducting research and disseminating research data to benefit individuals' everyday lives.

Regarding planning, technical progress facilitates the efficient retrieval of scientific sources (papers, reports, proceedings, monographs, etc.) for scientific investigation. Literature searches, which can be conducted electronically or in print, are now performed more quickly and effectively compared to historical experiences when physical travel was essential for finding books and journals. Specialized databases, such as OldMedline, Medline, PubMed, The Cochrane Library, EMBASE, BIOSIS, PsychINFO, and multidisciplinary databases like Clarivate Analytics, Scopus, Dialnet, and Latindex, are widely used. Supplementary information can also be found using Internet search engines like Scirus, Google Scholar, and SumSearch.[31]

Regarding realization, technical development has advanced our understanding of molecular biology, representing a turning point in our knowledge and linking it with bio-industrial advances. The history of science includes three types of discoveries: 1) those surprising both science and discoverers, 2) expected discoveries novel in their details, and 3) expected discoveries that came as a complete surprise.[32] From Mendel's laws of genetics (1865) to the DNA discovery (1869), DNA cloning (1972), DNA sequencing (1975), and the human genome sequence (2001), medicine has transformed from an empirical phenomenon into a scientific discipline. Consequently, bioinformatics has become a central research discipline in biomedical sciences, leading to new research directions such as comparative genomics, virtual evolution, metabolic networks, molecular 3D predictions, and morphometrics.[33]

Regarding dissemination, technical progress has enabled the development of modern health surveillance systems, which provide data to healthcare providers and public health agencies. These systems include healthcare provider networks (collecting longitudinal data and conducting studies on the incidence, prevalence, care, and outcomes of diseases), laboratory surveillance (using molecular epidemiological tools to study microbe types and monitor drug sensitivity), and disease registers (collecting information on diagnostic classification, treatment, and outcome). Websites like the Morbidity and Mortality Weekly Report (US CDC), Weekly Epidemiological Record (WHO), and European Eurosurveillance disseminate surveillance data.[34] The World Health Organization has formulated six criteria for a healthcare system: healthcare financing, service delivery, drugs and supplies, human resources, information, and healthcare management.[35]

An example of technological progress facilitating research dissemination and collaboration is GRISONET, created by the research group "Siglo de Oro" at the University of Navarra. This network connects internal and external academic members from Spanish and foreign universities and cultural institutions.[36] The blogosphere GRISOSFERA was also created to extend the research network and provide effective research opportunities, especially for doctoral students.[37]

Modern research is inherently international, with collaboration determining the diversity and complexity of research data. Technological development is rapid and multifaceted, making it impossible for a single research center to have the best material and human resources. Biomedical and social science research demands a wide variety of specialists and material supplies, facilitated by international research frameworks and projects. Research, financed by governmental and non-governmental organizations and private donations, seeks novel methods and approaches for understanding our world and human adaptation to changing environmental factors. Scientific investigations improve our understanding of human needs and lead to better disease management guidelines. The importance of technology in research was evident during the COVID-19 pandemic, where the creation of a new vaccine likely reduced infection complications. The internet provides easy access to the latest publications, helping to share recent research data and connect laboratories and research centers. Library catalogs, scientific databases, and laboratory webpages disseminate news on recent publications, building rich personal databases that create a strong methodological basis for ongoing and planned investigations.

Modern research is also transdisciplinary. Mixed methods research, widely used in contemporary investigations, supplies diverse methodological instruments to verify and triangulate research data. Overcoming the narrow areas of subjects and disciplines, *transdisciplinarity* cannot replace them; it represents "a scientific principle of work and organization" being a research principle and guiding problem perceptions, as well as their solution, without being solidified in theoretical forms. For this reason, *transdisciplinarity* is not considered to be a method or to be elaborated in the form of a methodology.[38]

Collaborating specialists from different scientific branches within a single research framework allows understanding phenomena from a complex perspective. Modern science, divided into many small branches and hybrid branches, analyzes scientific phenomena beyond the borders of specific fields, making possible the generalization of particular findings and formulating concrete recommendations for future studies. This modern, technological science allows the formation of new visions for rethinking previous research data and continuing research in a multidirectional perspective.

## Notes

1. Houssay, 1939, p. 19.
2. Brannan et al., 2012, pp. 583–584.
3. Benvenuto, 2019.
4. Alcántara, 2000.
5. Wolfe, 1972; Clark, 1983/1986, 1984/1987; Schwartzman, 1984, 1991; Pacheco, 1994; Altbach et al., 1989.
6. The first academies of sciences were founded in the 17th century: Académie Française in 1635 and Royal Society of London in 1660, a tendency that continued in the United States with the establishment of American Philosophical Society in Philadelphia in 1743 and John Adams' American Academy of Arts and Sciences in Boston in 1790, as well as the US National Academy of Sciences in 1863.
7. Dewey, 1916, p. 227.
8. Fuller, T. (ed.), 1989.
9. Habermas, 1987, pp. 19–20.
10. Ortega y Gasset, 1983.
11. Vernadsky, 1908/2002; 1911/2002.
12. If we observe the development of philosophical thought in modern Spain, we shall witness the brilliant continuation and elaboration of Ortega's ideas by contemporary researchers, published in journals edited by different Spanish universities (such as *Revista de Filosofía*; *Anales del Seminario de Historia de la Filosofía*; *Eikón/Imago*; *Escritura e Imagen*; *Ingenium. Revista Electrónica de Pensamiento Moderno y Metodología en Historia de las Ideas*; *Las Torres de Lucca. Revista Internacional de Filosofía Política*; *Logos. Anales del Seminario de Metafísica*; *Res Publica. Revista de Historia de las Ideas Políticas*, published by the Complutense University of Madrid; *Actas del Seminario de Historia de la Filosofía Española*, published by the University of Salamanca; *Daimon. Revista Internacional de Filosofía*, published by the University of Murcia; *Pensamiento. Revista de Investigación e Información Filosófica*, published by the Comillas Pontifical University; *Bajo Palabra*, published by the Autonomous University of Madrid; *Revista del Hispanismo Filosófico*, which reflects the prolific work of the members of the Hispanic Philosophical Association, to mention just a few).
13. <https://carnegieclassifications.iu.edu/>
14. Britt Arredondo, 2013.
15. Mittelstrass, 2018, pp. 57–59.

16. Prestigio editorial—SPI (<csic.es>)
17. Canetti, 1984; Le Bon, 2002; Meerloo, 2015.
18. París, 1984.
19. Ramón y Cajal, 1952.
20. Walliman, 2011.
21. On ethics: Broad, 1930; Singer, 1979; on Consequentialism: Pettit, 1993, 1997, 2000; Dreier, 1993; Portmore, 2007; on virtue ethics: Hooft (ed.), 2014; Louden, 1984; on Deontological ethics: Olson, 1967; Heuer, 2011; Lazar, 2017.
22. Merton, 1968; Tranøy, 1988, 1996.
23. Chubin, 1985.
24. Brannan et al., 2012, p. 621.
25. Readings, 1999, p. 53.
26. Guyatt, Drummond, 2002.
27. Mittelstrass, 2018, p. 55.
28. LaFollete, 1994.
29. Novikov and Novikov, 2013.
30. Hofmann, and Iversen, 2007; Walliman, 2011; Novikov and Novikov, 2013.
31. Haraldstad and Christophersen, 2007.
32. Mittelstrass, 2018, p. 22.
33. Fossum and Dissen, 2007.
34. Buehler and Kimball, 2015.
35. WHO (World Health Organization) (2007) *Everybody's business: Strengthening Health System to Improve Health Outcomes: WHO's Framework for Action*, Geneva: WHO.
36. Presentation. Group of Investigation Siglo de Oro (GRISO). University of Navarra (<unav.edu>)
37. Baraibar, Cohen, 2012.
38. Mittelstrass, 2018, p. 60.

## Bibliography

Alcántara, A. (2000), "Ciencia, conocimiento y sociedad en la investigación universitaria," *Perfiles Educativos*, XXII, 87, pp. 28–50.

Altbach, P. et al. (1989), *Scientific development and higher education: the case of newly industrializing nations*, New York: Praeger.

Baraibar, Á., Cohen, S. (2012), "Nuevas tecnologís y redes sociales en la investigación en Humanidades," *La perinola*, 16, pp. 155–164.

Benvenuto, G. (2019), "La responsibilidad social universitaria (RSU): un proyecto de investigación interuniversitario," *Cuestiones Pedagógicas*, 27, pp. 63–82.

Brannan, S., Chrispin, E., Davies, M., English, V., Mussell, R., Sheather, J., and Sommerville, A. (2012), *Medical ethics today: The BMA's handbook of ethics and law*. 3rd edition. Oxford: Blackwell Publishing.

Britt Arredondo, C. (2013), "De la Casa de Salomón a la Research University," *Revista Valenciana, estudios de filosofía y letras*, 11, pp. 69–89.

Broad, C. D. (1930), *Five types of ethical theory*, New York: Harcourt, Brace and Co.

Buehler, J. W. and Kimball, A. M. (2015), "Public health surveillance," in Roger Detels, Quarraisha Abdool Karim, Fran Baum, Liming Li, and Alastair H Leyland (eds.), *Oxford textbook of global public health*, Oxford: Oxford University Press, pp. 664–678.

Canetti, E. (1984), *Crowds and power*, New York: Farrar, Straus and Giroux.

Chubin, D. E. (1985), "Misconduct in research: An issue of science, policy, and practice," *Minerva*, 23, pp. 175–202.

Clark, B. R. (1983/1986), *The higher education system: academic organization in cross-national perspective*, Berkeley: University of California Press.

Clark, B. R. (1984/1987), *Perspectives on higher education: eight disciplinary and comparative views*, Berkeley: University of California Press.

Dewey, J. (1916), "The individual and the world," in John Dewey, *Democracy and education, the middle works 1899–1924*, vol. 9, Carbondale: Southern Illinois University Press, pp. 300–315.

Dreier, J. (1993), "The structure of normative theories," *Monist*, 76, pp. 22–40.

Fossum, S. and Dissen, E. (2007), "Methods in molecular biology," in Petter Laake, Haakon Breien Benestad, Bjorn R. Olsen (eds.), *Research methodology in the medical and biological sciences*, Amsterdam: Elsevier, pp. 161–197.

Fuller, T. (ed.) (1989), "THE IDEA OF A UNIVERSITY: 1950.," in *The voice of liberal learning: Michael Oakeshott on education*, New Haven and London: Yale University Press, pp. 95–104.

Guyatt, G., Drummond, R. (2002), *User's guides to the medical literature: a manual for evidence-based clinical practice*, Chicago: American Medical Association.

Habermas, J. (1987), "The idea of the University: Learning Processes," *New German Critique*, 41 (Special issue on the Critiques of the Enlightenment), pp. 3–22.

Haraldstad, A.-M. B. and Christophersen, E. (2007), "Literature search and personal reference databases," in Petter Laake, Haakon Breien Benestad, Bjorn R. Olsen (eds.), *Research methodology in the medical and biological sciences*, Amsterdam: Elsevier, pp. 125–160.

Heuer, U. (2011), "The paradox of deontology revisited," in Mark Timmons (ed.), *Oxford studies in normative ethics*, Oxford: Oxford University Press, pp. 236–267.

Hofmann, H. and Iversen, J-G. (2007), "Philosophy of science," in Petter Laake, Haakon Breien Benestad, Bjorn R. Olsen (eds.), *Research methodology in the medical and biological sciences*, Amsterdam: Elsevier, pp. 1–32.

Hooft, S. (ed.) (2014), *The handbook of virtue ethics*, Durham: Acumen Publishing Limited.

Houssay, B. (1939), "Recuerdos de un profesor y consideraciones sobre la investigación," in Marota, P., *El Profesor Bernardo A. Houssay (Discursos pronunciados con motivo de su designación como profesor honorario)*, Buenos Aires: Imprenta Universidad de Buenos Aires, pp. 11–27.

LaFollete, M. C. (1994), "The politics of research misconduct: Congressional oversight, universities, and science," *Journal of Higher Education*, 65, pp. 261–285.

Lazar, S. (2017), "Deontological decision theory and agent-centered options," *Ethics*, 127, pp. 579–609.

Le Bon, G. (2002), *The crowd. A study of the popular mind*, New York: Dover Publications.

Louden, R. (1984), "On some vices of virtue ethics," *American Philosophical Quarterly*, 21(3), pp. 227–236.

Meerloo, J. A. M. (2015), *The rape of the mind*, New York: Grosset & Dunlap.

Merton, R. (1968), *Social theory and social structure*, New York: Free Press.

Mittelstrass, J. (2018), *Theoria: chapters in the philosophy of science*, Berlin: De Gruyter.

Novikov, A. M. and Novikov D. A. (2013), *Research methodology. from philosophy of science to research design*, Amsterdam: CRC Press.

Olson, R. G. (1967), "Deontological ethics," in Paul Edwards (ed.), *The encyclopaedia of philosophy*, London: Collier Macmillan.

Ortega y Gasset, J. (1983), "Misión de la universidad," in José Ortega y Gasset, *Obras Completas*, vol. IV, pp. 313–353.

Pacheco, T. (1994), *La organización de la actividad científica en la UNAM*, México: CFSU-UNAM.

París, C. (1984), *Crítica de la civilización nuclear*, Madrid: Ediciones Libertarias.

Pettit, P. (1993), "Consequentialism," in Peter Singer (ed.), *A companion to ethics*, Oxford: Blackwell, pp. 230–240.

Pettit, P. (1997), "The consequentialist perspective," in Marcia W. Baron, Philip Pettit & Michael Slote, *Three methods of ethics*, Oxford: Blackwell, pp. 92–174.

Pettit, P. (2000), "Non-consequentialism and universalizability," *The Philosophical Quarterly*, 50, pp. 175–190.

Portmore, D. (2007), "Consequentializing moral theories," *Pacific Philosophical Quarterly*, 88, pp. 39–73.

Ramón y Cajal, S. (1952), *Los tónicos de la voluntad*, Madrid: Espasa-Calpe.

Readings, B. (1999), *The university in ruins*, Cambridge, MA: Harvard University Press.

Schwartzman, S. (1984), "The focus on scientific activity," in Burton Clark (ed.), *Perspectives on higher education: eight disciplinary and comparative views*, Berkeley: University of California Press, pp. 199–232.

Schwartzman, S. (1991), *A space for science: the development of the scientific community in Brazil*, University Park, PA: The Pennsylvania State University Press.

Singer, P. (1979), *Practical ethics*, Cambridge: Cambridge University Press.

Tranøy, K. E. (1988), *The moral import of science. Essays on normative theory, scientific activity and Wittengenstein*, Norway: Sigma Forlag.

Tranøy, K. E. (1996), "Ethical problems of scientific research: an action-theoretic approach," *The Monist*, 79, pp. 183–196.

Walliman, N. (2011), *Research methods. The basics*, London and New York: Routledge.

Wolfe, D. (1972), *The home of science: the role of the university*, New York: McGraw-Hill.

Vernadsky, V. (1908/2002), "Academic life," in Vladimir Vernadsky, *On science*, 2, Saint Petersburg: Russian Christian Humanitarian Institute, pp. 168–176.

Vernadsky, V. (1911/2002), "Crush," in Vladimir Vernadsky, *On science*, Saint Petersburg: Russian Christian Humanitarian Institute, pp. 177–181.

CHAPTER 4

# Modern University

## 4.1. Introduction

Our main approach to understanding universities is to examine their basic functions and describe the primary methods they use to achieve these functions. The word *university*, derived from the Latin *universitas*, signifies *universe* and *universality*. This implies that a university is a type of universe with its own organizational laws and that it creates a world of universalities that, in turn, conditions the formation of a cultural episteme, which generates and shares values throughout its existence.

According to Kant, the university is based on reason, which imparts its universality. The Kantian university emerged from a conflict between theology, medicine, and law on one side, and philosophy on the other. The relationship among these disciplines regulates the state–university relationship, fostering the development of the state while protecting the university from state power abuses.[1]

Historically, modern universities were characterized by an idea that served as their referent, as noted by Bill Readings: "Kant considered universities to be guided by *reason*, Humboldt by *culture*, and in recent times by the "techno-bureaucratic" notion of *excellence*. However, this latter notion lacks a referent: "excellence"—itself has no referent. The University of Excellence is the *simulacrum* of the idea of a university."[2]

The first universities were founded in Europe at the beginning of the eleventh century and were primarily teaching institutions where clerics and secular authorities offered students factual knowledge, as seen in Bologna, Paris, and Oxford. According to modern understanding, they were *teaching* universities whose scholars sometimes published their lectures, professional thoughts, or translations of Greek and Latin texts and commentaries. At the same time, universities served as support centers for individual researchers, as in the cases of Galileo Galilei at the University of Padua and Isaac Newton at Cambridge University. It was only from the nineteenth century that *research* universities began to appear, first in Germany and later in the United States.[3]

The transformation of teaching universities into research institutions occurred early in the nineteenth century, mostly in the field of humanities, particularly classical languages. With the foundation of the University of Berlin in 1809, university staff shifted their focus to research, especially in philology and linguistics. In natural science, Justus Liebig was the first to establish a scientific laboratory in 1826, a trend that became more noticeable with technological development and the unification of Germany in 1870.[4]

From the very beginning, German universities carried the idea of educating through research, understanding the role of science-based education in the formation of individuals, societies, and nations. From this moment, the state was considered a guarantor of the university mission: freedom of teaching and research.[5]

Emerging as a core idea for the organization of universities, *Bildung*[6] or *edification* found its place at the center of German cultural episteme from the eighteenth century until the mid-twentieth century. *Wissenschaft* or *science* was considered to have a research basis oriented by truth and represented a process for capturing totality, resulting in the formation of another, more precise terminological definition of the phenomenon—*Wissenschaftlichkeit* or "systematic enquiry driven by 'the spirit of truth.'"[8] This was the historical origin of the idea of the university—"science through research and education through science," characterizing universities as having an attitude and duty toward truth.[9]

The foundation of Harvard College in 1636 and the establishment of US universities according to the German model fostered the development of a research culture in the United States. This led to many scientific innovations, including the foundation of Jefferson Physical Laboratory in the early 1870s and the first American research university, Johns Hopkins University, in 1876. This was followed by the establishment of other universities, particularly Clark University in 1889, Stanford University in 1891, and the University of Chicago in 1892.[10]

The history of university foundations in Japan and China is also notable. In Japan, the University of Tokyo was founded in the 1870s, followed by the establishment of imperial universities by the 1920s, including the universities of Hokkaido, Tohoku, Nagoya, Kyoto, Osaka, Kyushu, Seoul, and Taipei. By the late 1990s, their number had increased to 100. In China, the foundation of universities based on Western models began in the late nineteenth century. After the establishment of the People's Republic of China in 1949, the Soviet Union's model was adopted, leading to the establishment of the Chinese Academy of

Sciences, which conducted all research, while universities functioned merely as teaching institutions. Only in 1978 did educational reforms broaden university curricula and make space for research, with Peking and Tsinghua universities creating graduate schools following the US model.[11]

Different philosophers and university representatives have cultivated interesting ideas regarding the mission of universities. Among them are Vladimir Vernadsky, José Ortega y Gasset, and Bertrand Russell.

Vladimir Vernadsky, in his texts "Academic Life" and "Crush," discussed three basic functions of universities: 1) teaching what has already been discovered by human thinking, 2) training young generations to think scientifically and conduct research, representing centers for independent scientific research, and 3) disseminating new knowledge into society, as well as forming new ways of working and thinking.[12]

Ortega y Gasset described the mission of higher education as: a) teaching intellectual professions, and b) scientific investigation and the formation of future researchers. According to Ortega, human life is chaotic and full of confusion; people try to survive and seek ways out in order not to be lost. In other words, they look for clear and valid ideas about the universe and positive convictions about things and the surrounding world, which can be defined as culture. According to Ortega, the university is the place where an individual's contemporary culture or system of values is taught. Thus, in addition to teaching professions and conducting scientific investigations, Ortega added another component and defined the main functions of higher education as follows: a) transmission of culture, b) teaching of professions, and c) scientific investigation and the education of a new generation of researchers.[13]

Bertrand Russell briefly described the history of British universities and identified three stages of their development: first, when they served as training colleges for clergy; second, during the Renaissance, when the so-called "education of a gentleman" became accepted; and third, when universities became training schools for the professions. Russell noted that universities have two purposes: to train individuals for certain professions and to facilitate both teaching and research, the latter being especially important when discussing the role of universities in the life of humanity.[14] In "Science and Values," Bertrand Russell indicates that "The sphere of values lies outside science, except in so far as science consists in the pursuit of knowledge. Science as the pursuit of power must not obtrude upon the sphere of values, and scientific technique, if it is to enrich human life, must not outweigh the ends which it should serve."[15]

Indeed, the creation of new knowledge, as well as its transmission and dissemination, is based on ethical grounds that determine a) the necessity of teaching ethics (ethics education) and b) the development of professional ethics that promote academic citizenship. The first involves familiarizing students with basic ethical theories (consequentialist ethics, communitarian ethics, deontological ethics, the "four principles approach" to ethics, narrative ethics, and virtue ethics). The second involves understanding the role of ethics in the formation of a professional. Both are necessary steps for forming academic citizenship, which refers to the role performed by individuals in creating modern civic society. This is described in the Dutch law on higher education (article 1.3.5), which states that "[...] universities do not only have the legal duty to educate the academic qualities of their students, but the state also expects them to contribute to the personal development of students as well as the students' sense of responsibility for the well-being of society, which might be called academic citizenship."[16]

The historical development of different ideas on education, as well as the introduction of novel methods of teaching and learning, demonstrate the value-driven nature of modern universities. Even though the COVID-19 pandemic limited physical interaction between teachers and students, education continues to deepen its traditional social function: innovative methods in education, including peer instruction, computer-assisted instruction, and others, represent special research interests for social science professionals. Various investigations address this topic, such as the study of pre-class reading behavior using *Perusall*, which indicated higher reading assignment completion rates compared to those reported in the literature (90–95 percent of students completed reading assignments before classes versus 60–80 percent reported by other studies).[17]

Research is another value with an ethical dimension. Different types of scientific misconduct highlight the lack of moral grounding in research and the necessity of ethics education for young researchers. At the same time, to create an ethical environment at the university, the organization of university life should be based on a solid ethical foundation. Increased teaching loads, attempts to reduce financial resources for research activities by university authorities, and rising standards in the number of publications required in top-rated journals do not facilitate a positive university climate.[18]

Academic citizenship shapes the formation of ethically oriented individuals within academia and their professional ethical projection outside it. Modern universities should play a decisive role in cultivating civic values that contribute to the well-being of society and form a fundamental basis for the happiness of its members. Respect and tolerance for the members of a modern multicultural society are major values to be discussed and explained to students. Filled with mutual respect, modern universities foster the creation of a friendly and respectful environment for the social functions of their members.

Public health research at universities offers a set of possibilities that determine the production of value-oriented and evidence-based knowledge.[19] The growing trend toward new diagnostic methods and the development of optimal treatment approaches require planning and conducting transdisciplinary and funded research with the participation of university-affiliated staff and biomedical students.[20] By linking research products with societal needs, universities are well-positioned to take advantage of a new social agreement: they create and share values that respond to modern challenges. Thus, research itself becomes one of the main values that necessitate the formation of other values, whether cultural or scientific. The formation, transmission, and dissemination of new and value-driven knowledge condition the equal distribution of material and non-material benefits, creating tolerant and responsible citizens for the modern civic community.

## 4.2. Modern University: Education and Research Mediated by Technological Progress

Modern universities are multifunctional centers dedicated to teaching and research, as well as the cultivation and sharing of values related to societal well-being. Contemporary challenges, shaped by a wide range of public health demands, determine the rapid transformation of academia and the emergence of novel circumstances that affect how people live and work. Social and political fluctuations producing migration from low-income to middle-income countries lead to the formation of multicultural societies with different preferences and perceptions of the surrounding world. Together with economic characteristics, migration also changes the public health systems in host countries—after all, people travel with their microflora, and the health system in developing countries in the twenty-first century leaves much to be desired. Healthcare in our century is a complex phenomenon, combining knowledge from biomedical and social sciences. Particular attention is paid to the study of communicable diseases and the social causes of their development, such as migration, rapid urban growth, and industrialization. The social distancing policy, which may play a crucial role in preventing the spread of communicable diseases, was adopted as an essential measure to curb the spread of COVID-19, forcing universities to reconsider traditional methods of functioning.

The tradition of online learning dates back to the 1980s,[21] facilitating the export of higher education and simplifying matters related to technical, financial, and travel issues. This experience resulted in a certain preparedness at the onset of the COVID-19 pandemic, allowing universities to shift from in-person learning (sharing the same physical classroom by students and lecturers) to distance education, also known as online learning (joining the class from different locations). Distance education can be synchronous, where all participants interact in real-time, or asynchronous, where lectures are recorded, and students watch them at their convenience. Another form of distance education is *emergency remote education*, which requires teachers to "quickly adapt their pedagogical activity to a virtual environment."[22]

However, the shift from in-person learning to online learning was not as smooth as expected.[23] Digital transformation, which relies on the digital competencies of university staff and students[24] and the accessibility of technical facilities by broad segments of society, revealed different perceptions[25] and almost revolutionary changes in curricular activity.[26] Major difficulties related to digital competencies were observed in countries most affected by the COVID-19 pandemic.[27] Probably the most productive method of learning in today's complex reality is *blended learning*,[28] representing various forms of classroom and online educational approaches, including *hybrid learning* (with half the students in a class and the other half online)[29] or the use of *"mirror rooms"* (face-to-face classes at a safe distance).[30]

One way for the development of modern universities is long-term academic partnerships, offering excellent and promising possibilities for educational and research institutions in developing countries. Improving teaching and research, as well as infrastructural and technological facilities, academic collaboration can lead to successful curricular reform and innovation resulting in professional achievements and academic excellence.[31]

Technical progress facilitates the development of sciences that inform the health arena, offering diverse and complex sources for collecting and analyzing research data, such as the creation of a system of vital statistics, possibilities of conducting population surveys, gathering information on disease surveillance, and creating administrative databases, registers, and electronic health records databases.

## 4.3. Public Health Research: University and Values

The organization and implementation of research procedures are vital across various fields of knowledge. However, a particularly pressing necessity is understanding the basis of human diseases, their biology, and pathology, along with developing treatment approaches and preventive measures. Aim-driven research protocols, a statistically sufficient number of patients for clinical trials, external review of research design, and continuous surveillance are essential for conducting contemporary scientific research. These measures result in producing new knowledge that benefits future patients.[32]

Health investigation is a crucial tool for understanding, predicting, and improving population health. According to the 2014–2020 European Union strategy,[33] research plays a pivotal role in economic and social development through innovation.[34] Significant funding has been allocated for medical research, facilitating the treatment and prevention of various diseases. Medical universities are key contributors to the accumulation, transmission, and dissemination of theoretical and clinical knowledge.[35] They teach students innovative methods of disease evaluation and develop practical and scientific skills within any health policy agenda.[36]

The development of health systems requires the transformation of research-based interventions.[37] Population health intervention research, inherently contextualized, focuses on preventive approaches and technological and organizational innovations. The national public health research program announced in France in August 2017 embodies the idea that "[...] funded research contributes to the national aims to invest in health prevention, to improve the efficacy and efficiency of the health system, and to reduce health inequalities."[38] Health communication[39] is a crucial tool for informing society about the main aspects of health-related topics.[40] Effective health communication enhances health literacy, enabling individuals to understand and use information about key health issues such as disease prevention, morbidity rates, and vaccination.[41]

One modern method of health communication is publication. Historical methods of exchanging information such as carving on stone, smoke signals, papyrus, couriers, and newspapers are now outdated. The fundamental needs of communication—disseminating information, education, and relationship building—demand novel methods and refinement of existing ones. Among these, the role of scientific publication is significant.[42]

A primary goal of public health research is to elevate society's education level and help individuals become healthier, more civilized, and tolerant.[43] Regarding health issues, three types of knowledge can be identified: *lay knowledge*, which refers to non-professional opinions on medical issues based on personal and historical experience; *biomedical knowledge*, which is social scientific knowledge; and *social science knowledge*, which places "the social" at the center of research and understanding morbidity and mortality. Health research requires a complex set of instruments, and the variety of investigation methods can make its implementation challenging. While in the twentieth century, the term *research* referred to pure scientific acts, contemporary research includes the collective inquiry of participants involved in the prevention, treatment, and rehabilitation of various pathological conditions. This is how *qualitative* approaches have complemented *quantitative* ones, forming mixed-method (simultaneous, sequential, or emergent) research programs to inform the health arena. Mixed methods are used in health services, psychiatry, aging research, and nursing, among other fields.[44] Regardless of the research methods used, all serve *exploratory*, *descriptive*, and *explanatory* purposes. Different methods are distinguished by "a) the type of research question used, b) the extent of control an investigator has over actual behavioral events, c) the degree of focus on contemporary as opposed to historical events."[45]

As science knows no borders, the international nature of modern scientific investigation is one of its main strengths. International collaboration involves a diverse spectrum of researchers and facilitates the effective exchange of newly created knowledge, as well as the formation of universal civic values. Intellectual generosity and open access to published papers are key drivers of innovative and value-determined science. International projects promote the effective utilization of results and familiarization with cultural diversity, which should be considered in modern biomedical research. Cultural diversity, based on values shared by specific societies or populations, plays a crucial role in understanding differences in morbidity and mortality, developing public health approaches, and formulating culture-specific recommendations. Dietary preferences, physical activity, sedentary lifestyles, and other public health issues are culture-mediated, shaped by different lifestyle traditions.

Value-based research is increasingly important as multidisciplinary approaches enable different countries to communicate and discover new research perspectives on disease treatment and prevention. Building a healthy society remains a priority for creating a flexible public health model that can be adapted to different cultural contexts. Considering humans as beings composed of molecules, tissues, and organs, as well as social and spiritual beings, necessitates a complex approach to understanding the philosophy of health. This approach aims to find new medical and cultural ways of understanding the philosophy of biomedical sciences. Four basic principles of medical ethics should be strictly followed during clinical investigations: respect for patient autonomy, beneficence (promoting what is best for the patient), non-maleficence (avoiding harm), and justice (including distributive justice, respect for the law, rights, and retributive justice).[46]

### 4.3.1. Benefits of University Research in Public Health

Universities offer the opportunity to conduct research across all preclinical and clinical departments.[47] A huge number of medical professionals worldwide are affiliated with medical schools or university hospitals, providing universities with the necessary human resources for planning and conducting scientific investigations.[48] Additionally, laboratories and clinical centers are equipped with modern facilities that need to be effectively integrated into the research plan. The combination of both human and technical resources makes universities an attractive environment for research.[49] Public health research is intricately linked with clinical medicine, encompassing a complex scientific dimension not only at the population or health services level but also at the clinical level.[50] To prevent and treat diseases, public health research connects epidemiology with health services and social and environmental sciences with clinical research. It's no coincidence that the European Union allocated approximately 8 percent of its budget to research during 2014–2020.[51] One of the main focal points of the European Public Health Association is research propelled by Public Health Innovation and Research in Europe.[52] In European countries, national research systems are overseen by Ministries of Science and Ministries of Education. Ministries of Science often consider public health research to be the prerogative of Ministries of Health.[53] Consequently, Ministries of Health generally fund national schools of public health to teach public health sciences and conduct research. The primary venue for the development of the modern public health agenda is typically found in medical schools, universities, and institutes.[54]

Two additional considerations may be added to the points mentioned above: firstly, universities represent a hub of students who need to develop not only teaching but also research skills; secondly, emeritus professors who do not actively participate in everyday clinical procedures can share their knowledge and experience with younger colleagues. The combination of these factors provides benefits for all members of the medical society.

One of the main benefits of university medical research is that health research requires knowledge from various sciences (social and biomedical) to be conducted.[55] A transdisciplinary approach to scientific evaluation is modern and highly productive.[56] Experimental investigations merge theory with practice, utilizing different branches of biological and physical sciences to explain pathological changes in the human body. Employing both *quantitative* and *qualitative* research methods guarantees the accumulation of evidence necessary for understanding the scientific, social, and cultural complexities within which the health system operates. University departments and their libraries provide ample opportunities for interdisciplinary research.[57]

To conduct scientific research, it is necessary to attract corresponding funds. Grant providers at national and international levels demand institutions to provide firm assurance for investigation. From this perspective, universities are among the most trustworthy institutions capable of planning and conducting research. The high quality of affiliated professionals, along with diverse and innovative medical curricula implemented by medical schools, ensures the continuous progress of university research. Simultaneously, universities can structure their own scientific budget (self-funding), organizing pilot studies as the initial step of research to attract more complex and substantial financing.[58]

It is further assumed that the results of scientific investigations serve as a valid source of knowledge for the formation of clinical recommendations, as widely practiced during the COVID-19 pandemic. University hospitals can utilize the results of clinical trials in everyday practice, reducing treatment complications, eliminating hospital infections, improving rehabilitation procedures, and accumulating new clinical knowledge. Physicians, nurses, and allied medical staff base their work on research knowledge, underscoring the importance of research while providing everyday medical services. Thus, universities with their hospitals are among the primary beneficiaries of scientific research.

Research results at the university level may be presented, collected, and shared through various channels. Alongside traditional channels such as print and broadcast media, new communication methods have emerged. In our era of rapid technological advancements and modern communication facilities, Internet technologies are the most rapid and cost-effective tools for reaching societies and populations.[59] Social media, digital technologies, and preprint databases facilitate the exchange of professional information. However, even in today's accelerated world of technocratic challenges, one of the most rigorous and effective methods of professional communication remains the publication of scientific articles. Although participation in congresses and clinical visits offers unique opportunities to exchange personal and professional experiences, publication in peer-reviewed journals is crucial for the formation of specialists with both theoretical and practical skills. All the aforementioned reasons highlight the advantages of university research.[60]

A university is part of *culture*, representing a complex component distinct from teaching and research.[61] Max Scheler offered a classical description of a cultural individual, distinguishing them from an intelligent person or researcher. Indeed, what matters is not the number of books one reads, as debated by ancient Greek philosophers, but how much one succeeds in integrating their reading into everyday life. There are two ways to the formation of a responsible citizen: one may spend many hours reading, with the next step being the application of what they read to their actions, thereby shaping their personal character; or personal character may be formed throughout life and enriched by reading. Both paths exemplify the formation of a person with inherently ethical values. However, it is rare for an uneducated individual lacking a habit of action to be ethically oriented; and if they are, it is an exception or a coincidence resulting from certain events in their life, not solely due to the realization of their free will.

Those involved in university life create, transmit, and disseminate new knowledge. The aim of this process is to discover and uphold the truth, which forms the foundation for social equality. Hence, university life is based on the possibilities of professional and social self-realization, aiming to stimulate individuals to develop their inner potential for the betterment of their micro-societies. This is achievable through research activities that provide a solid foundation for the scientific and technical advancement of societies, enabling the transformation of research products into applicable everyday tools. Here, research intersects with society, shaping its development and creating new perspectives for a better understanding of modern challenges that are not only material but also spiritual in nature. Ethical and aesthetic characteristics of a modern individual are developed within the framework of new necessities arising from contemporary lifestyles and interpersonal relations. Intellectual development should lead to the formation of internal freedom, facilitating the acceptance of different cultures and fostering tolerant approaches to the needs of other individuals, ethnic groups, and nations. These factors contribute to the development of social and political systems seeking peaceful resolutions to complex conflicts, including military ones.

Education is a necessity, yet it should not be confined to rigid schemes or inflexible curricular plans. We have a wealth of experience in organizing university life within different cultural paradigms. Our main focus should be on creating an atmosphere conducive to productivity for both university personnel and students. Modern types of academic contracts and current research possibilities can meet the basic demands of university members to be productive and successful. Sabbatical years, which provide a valuable opportunity to conclude extensive research or plan and execute new projects, should be widely utilized by universities to promote the publishing careers of researchers. Publishing not only disseminates new ideas but also enhances the recognition of universities worldwide. Special financial support for publishing, as well as support for visits to various international research centers, will foster the development of researchers with contemporary perspectives on the current nature of scientific challenges. International collaboration stands as one of the most significant achievements of universities, contributing to the production of multiperspective and multifunctional research products.

And finally, modern universities play a crucial role in shaping individuals with an ethically oriented character, laying the foundation for the concept of a responsible citizen who is respectful to their society and responsive to the new challenges society faces. Values and ethics, rooted in basic human needs, influence the understanding of human equality and underscore the necessity of enhancing the quality of life in different countries worldwide. It is now evident that material resources alone are insufficient for eradicating poverty and that education alone cannot guarantee societal well-being. What we observe in our contemporary world is a stagnation of thinking and a lack of respect for other cultures and nationalities. Aggression, military intervention, and the erosion of interpersonal relations may lead to the development of modern humanitarian crises, resulting in a misunderstanding of basic human rights and values. Only through social responsibility can we foster a friendly atmosphere in the complex modern world of human behavior.

## Notes

1. Kant, 1992.
2. Readings, 1999, p. 54.
3. Atkinson and Blanpied, 2008.
4. Ibid.
5. Maarten, 2006.
6. On *Bildung*, see Masschelein and Ricken, 2003.
7. On differences between the terminological meaning of "science" in German and English, see Maarten, 2006, p. 37; Sadegh-Zadeh, 2015, vol. 2, pp. 856–864.
8. Maarten, 2006, pp. 31, 38.
9. Ibid., p. 38.
10. Atkinson and Blanpied, 2008.
11. Ibid.
12. Vernadsky, 1908/2002, 1911/2002.
13. Ortega, 1983, pp. 319–326.
14. Russell, 2010, pp. 191–197.
15. Russell, 2009, p. 200.
16. De Ruyter and Schinkel, 2017, p. 126.
17. Miller et al., 2018.
18. París, 1983; Roberts, 2013; De Ruyter and Schinkel, 2017; Gibbs, 2017.
19. On philosophy of evidence-based medicine in general, and on the EBM "hierarchies" in particular, see Howick: "The philosophy of evidence-based medicine is best expressed in the EBM 'hierarchies': 1) Randomized trials (RCTs), or systematic reviews of many randomized trials, generally offer stronger evidential support than observational studies; 2) comparative clinical

studies in general (including both RCTs and observational studies) offer stronger evidential support than "mechanistic" reasoning ('pathophysiologic rationale') from more basic sciences; 3) comparative clinical studies in general offer stronger evidential support than expert clinical judgement" (Howick, 2011, p. 4).

20. Two types of *transdisciplinarity* is detected regarding the problems it makes reference to: one is the so-called *practical transdisciplinarity*, that makes reference to problems foreign to science, and another is *theoretical transdisciplinarity*, that finds its origin in more strictly scientific problems (Mittelstrass, 2018, p. 65).
21. Babatunde and Soykan, 2020.
22. Verde and Valero, 2021.
23. Arkorful and Abaidoo, 2015.
24. Ferrari, 2012.
25. Bond et al., 2018.
26. Hiltz and Turoff, 2005; Means et al., 2009.
27. Valdivia, 2020.
28. Heilporn et al., 2021.
29. Bao, 2020.
30. Verde and Valero, 2021.
31. Mulvihill and Debas, 2011.
32. Brannan et al., 2012, pp. 583–584.
33. European Commission. *Europe 2020: A strategy for smart, sustainable and inclusive growth.* Brussels, 2010. COM (2010) 2020 final, cited in Mark McCarthy and Dineke Zeegers Paget (2013), "Public health innovation and research in Europe: introduction to the supplement," *Eur J Public Health* (Suppl. 2), pp. 2–5.
34. David, Sizer, 2003; Núñez Delicado, 2015.
35. Thier, 1992; Springer and Genat, 2004.
36. Norman, 2011.
37. Hart and Bond, 1995.
38. François and Cambon, 2017.
39. On the topic of health communication, especially on the organization of the various approaches to culture in health communication, see Dutta and Basu, 2011, pp. 320–334.
40. Schiavo, 2007; Cline, 2013.

41. Phoenix, 2010.
42. Seidman et al., 2013. Historically, first three professional medical journals were *New England Journal of Medicine* (started in 1812), *Lancet* (from 1823) and *The Journal of American Medical Association* (started in 1883).
43. González Rincón and Arcángel Urbina, 2013.
44. Creswell, 2014.
45. Yin, 2003.
46. Hope, 2004.
47. Blanco Jiménez and Blanco Jiménez, 2000.
48. Probst et al., 2007.
49. Conde Guerri, 2001; Walteros, 2008.
50. Barnhoorn et al., 2013.
51. European Commission. *A Budget for Europe*. Brussels 2011, COM (2011) 500. Final.
52. Zeegers Paget et al., 2013.
53. Conceição et al., 2013.
54. Conceição et al., 2009.
55. McCarthy, 2011; McCarthy and Zeegers Paget, 2013.
56. On the concepts of interdisciplinarity and transdisciplinarity, see Mittelstrass 1987, 2003, 2018.
57. Remedios Moralejo Álvarez, 1996; Abadal and Güell, 2006.
58. Veatch et al., 2010. On this topic, see *Theory and research in promoting public health*, S. Earle, C. E. Lloyd, M. Sidell and S. Spurr (eds.), London: Sage Publications in association with The Open University, 2007.
59. Cabrero Almenara et al., 2009.
60. Chaves García and Arias Rodríguez, 1998.
61. "The process of hermeneutic reworking is called culture, and it has a double articulation. On the one hand, culture names an *identity*. It is the unity of all knowledges that are the object of study; it is the object of *Wissenschaft* (scientific-philosophical study). On the other hand, culture names a *process of development*, of the cultivation of character—*Bildung*. In the modern University, the two branches of this process are research and teaching, and the particularity of the Idealists was to insist that the specificity of the University comes from the fact that it is the place where the two are inseparable" (Readings, 1999, p. 64)

# Bibliography

Abadal, E., Güell, C. (2006), "Investigadores en el campus: recursos y servicios para la investigación en la biblioteca universitaria," *Mi biblioteca: La revista del mundo bibliotecario*, 4, pp. 64–71.

Arkorful, V. and Abaidoo, N. (2015), "The role of e-learning, advantages and disadvantages of its adoption in higher education," *International Journal of Instructional Technology and Distance Learning*, 12 (1), pp. 29–42.

Atkinson, R. C. and W. A. Blanpied (2008), "Research universities: core of the US science and technology system," *Technology in Society*, 30, pp. 30–48.

Babatunde A., O. and Soykan, E. (2020), "Covid-19 pandemic and online learning: the challenges and opportunities," *Interactive Learning Environments*, 31(2), pp. 863–875.

Bao, W. (2020), "COVID-19 and online teaching in higher education: a case study of Peking University," *Hum. Behav. Emerg. Technol.*, 2, pp. 113–115.

Barnhoorn, F., McCarthy, M., Devillé, W., Alexanderson, K., Voss, M., Conceição, C. (2013), "PHIRE (Public Health Innovation and Research in Europe): methods, structures and evaluation," *Eur. J. Public Health*, 23 (Suppl. 2), pp. 6–11.

Blanco Jiménez, A., Blanco Jiménez, F. (2000), "La investigación universitaria: aspectos científicos y jurídicos," *Esic market*, 106, pp. 23–37.

Bond, M. M., Dolch, V. I., Bedenlier, C. S., and Zawacki-Richter, O. (2018),"Digital transformation in German higher education: Student and teacher perceptions and usage of digital media," *International Journal of Educational Technology in Higher Education*, 15 (1), p. 48.

Brannan, S., Chrispin, E., Davies, M., English, V., Mussell, R., Sheather, J., and Sommerville, A. (2012), *Medical ethics today: the BMA's handbook of ethics and law*. 3rd edition. Oxford: Blackwell Publishing.

Cabrero Almenara, J., Román Graván, P., Del Carmen Llorente Cejudo, M. (2009), "La investigación sobre e-learning: aportaciones para su incorporación a la formación universitaria," *Educare*, 13, 1, pp.10–35.

Chaves García, R., Arias Rodríguez, A. (1998), "La investigación universitaria en España: situación actual y perspectivas," *Hacienda Pública Española*, N. Extra, pp. 179–206.

Cline, R. (2013), *American Public Health Association (APHA) Health communication Working Group brochure*, cited in Seidman, C. S., Silberg, W. M, Patrik, K. (2013), "Contemporary issues in scientific communication and public health education," in James W. Holsinger Jr. (ed.), *Contemporary public health*, Kentucky: The University Press of Kentucky, pp. 171–192.

Conceição, C., Lenadro, A., McCarthy, M. (2009), "National support to public health research: a survey of European ministries," *BMC Public Health*, 9, p. 203.

Conceição, C., Grimaud, O., McCarthy, M., Barnhoorn, F., Sammut, M., Saliba, A., Katreniakova, Z., Narkauskaité, L. (2013), "Programmes and calls for public health research in European countries," *Eur. J. Public Health*, 23 (Suppl. 2), pp. 30–34.

Conde Guerri, B. (2001), "Apuntes sobre la investigación universitaria," *Trébede: Mensual aragonés de análisis, opinion y cultura*, 57, pp. 71–75.

Creswell J. (2014), *Research design. Qualitative, quantitative, and mixed methods approach*, Thousand Oaks, CA: Sage.

David, W., Sizer, J. (2003), "Innovación e investigación universitaria en la sociedad del conocimiento: la experiencia escocesa," in: Josep María Vilalta, Eduard Pallejá (coords.), *Universidades y desarrollo territorial en la sociedad del conocimiento*, Diputación de Barcelona: Universidad Politécnica de Barcelona, pp. 71–93.

De Ruyter, D. and Schinkel, A. (2017), "Ethics education at the university: from teaching an ethics module to education for the good life," *Bordón*, 69 (4), pp. 125–138.

Dutta, M. J. and Basu, A. (2011), "Culture, communication, and health. A guiding framework," in Teresa L. Thompson, Roxanne Parrott, and John F. Nussbaum (eds.), *The Routledge handbook of health communication*, 2nd ed., New York: Routledge.

Ferrari, A. (2012), *Digital competence in practice: An analysis of frameworks*, Luxembourg: Publication Office of the European Union.

François, A., Cambon, L. (2017), "Transformation of health systems: contribution of population health intervention research," *The Lancet Public Health*, 2, pp. e539.

Gibbs, P. (2017), *Why universities should seek happiness and contentment?* London: Bloomsbury.

González Rincón, O., Arcángel Urbina, R. (2013), "Investigación universitaria herramienta de transformación social," *Revista de Formación Gerencial*, 12, 1, pp. 193–210.

Hart, E. and Bond, M. (1995), *Action research for health and social care: A guide to practice*, Buckingham, UK: Open University Press.

Heilporn, G., Lakhal, S., and Bélisle, M. (2021), "An examination of teachers' strategies to foster student engagement in blended learning in higher education," *Int. J. Educ. Technol.*, 51, pp. 1117–1135.

Hiltz, S. R. and Turoff, M. (2005), "Education goes digital: The evolution of online learning and the revolution in higher education," *Communications of the ACM*, 48 (10), pp. 59–64.

Hope, T. (2004), *Medical ethics. A very short introduction*, New York: Oxford UP.

Howick, J. (2011), *The Philosophy of Evidence-Based Medicine*, Oxford: Wiley-Blackwell.

Kant, I. (1992), *The conflict of the faculties*, Lincoln: University of Nebraska Press.

Maarten, S. (2006), "'Education through research' at European Universities: notes on the orientation of academic research," *Journal of Philosophy of Education*, 40 (1), pp. 31–50.

Masschelein, J. and N. Ricken (2003), "Do we (still) need the concept of Bildung," *Educational Philosophy and Theory*, 35 (2), pp. 139–154.

McCarthy, M. (2011), "Health research: Europe's future," *Lancet*, 377, pp. 1744–1745.

McCarthy, M. and Zeegers Paget, D. (2013), "Public health innovation and research in Europe: introduction to the supplement," *Eur J Public Health* (Suppl. 2), pp. 2–5.

Means, B., Toyama, Y., Murphy, R., Bakia, M., and Jones, K. (2009), "Evaluation of evidence-based practices in online learning: a meta-analysis and review of online learning studies," US Department of Education: Office of Planning, Evaluation, and Policy Development Policy and Program Studies Service.

Miller, K., Lukoff, B., King, G. and Mazur, E. (2018), "Use of a social annotation platform for pre-class reading assignments in a flipped introductory physics class," *Front. Educ.*, 3, pp. 8.

Mittelstrass, J. (1987), "Die Stunde der Interdisziplinaritaet?," in Jürgen Kocka (ed.), *Interdisziplinaritaet: Praxis – Herausforderung – Ideologie*, Frankfurt: Suhrkamp, pp. 152–158.

Mittelstrass, J. (2003), *Transdisziplinaritaet – wissenschaftliche Zukunft und institutionelle Wirklichkeit*, Konstanz: Universitaetsverlag.

Mittelstrass, J. (2018), *Theoria: chapters in the philosophy of science*, Berlin: De Gruyter, 2018.

Mulvihill, J. D. and Debas, H. I. (2011), "Long-term academic partnership for capacity building in health in developing countries," in Richard Parker and Marni Sommer (eds.), *Routledge handbook of global public health*, London and New York: Routledge, pp. 506–515.

Norman, G. (2011), "Fifty years of medical education research: waves of migration," *Med. Educ.*, 45(8), pp. 85–91.

Núñez Delicado, E. (2015), *"Relación investigación-innovación educativa universitaria,"* in Juan José González Ortiz, Ana González Báidez (coords.), *La Universidad como comunidad de innovación y cambio*, Murcia: Fundación Universitaria San Antonio, pp. 60–67.

Ortega y Gasset, J., (1983), "Misión de la universidad," in José Ortega y Gasset, *Obras Completas*, vol. IV, pp. 313–353.

París, C. (1983), *Lección inaugural del curso académico 1983–1984*, Madrid: Ciudad Universitaria de Cantoblanco.

Phoenix, D. (2010), "The importance of educational research," *Journal of Biological Education*, 33, pp. 2–3.

Probst, C., de Weert, E., and Witte, J. (2007), "Medical education in Bachelor-Master structure: the Swiss model," cited in EUA Bologna-Handbook: *Making Bologna work*, Raabe: Berlin, pp. 1–20.

Readings, B. (1999), *The university in ruins*, Cambridge, MA: Harvard University Press.

Remedios Moralejo Álvarez, M. (1996), "Investigación de la Biblioteca Universitaria Española: Estado de la cuestión," *Boletín de la ANABAD*, 46, 3–4, pp. 9–34.

Roberts, P. (2013), "Happiness, despair and education," *Studies in Philosophy and Education*, 32, pp. 463–475.

Russell, B. (2009), "Science and values," in Bertrand Russell, *The Scientific outlook*, London and New York: Routledge, pp. 195–202.

Russell, B. (2010), "The university," in Bertrand Russell, *On education*, London and New York: Routledge, pp. 190–197.

Sadegh-Zadeh, K. (2015), *Handbook of analytic philosophy of medicine*. 2 vols., 2nd edition. Dordrecht: Springer.

Schiavo, R. (2007), *Health communication: from theory to practice*, San Francisco: Jossey-Bass.

Seidman C. S., Silberg, W. M., Patrik, K. (2013), "Contemporary issues in scientific communication and public health education," in James W. Holsinger Jr. (ed.), *Contemporary Public Health*, Kentucky: The University Press of Kentucky.

Springer, E., Genat, W. (2004), *Action research in health*, New Jersey: Pearson.

Thier, S. O. (1992), "Preventing the decline of academic medicine," *Acad. Med.*, 67, 11, pp. 731–737.

Valdivia, P. (2020), "Apuntes sobre covid-19 y desigualidad: el derecho a la educación," in Rodrigo Browne and Carlos del Valle (eds.), *La comunicación en tiempos de pandemia*, Temuco: Ediciones Universidad de la Frontera, pp. 15–18.

Veatch R. M., Haddad, A. M., English, D. C. (2010), *Case studies in biomedical ethics*, New York: Oxford University Press.

Verde, A. and Valero, J. M. (2021), "Teaching and learning modalities in higher education during the pandemic: responses to coronavirus disease 2019 from Spain," *Front. Psychol.*, 12: 648592.

Vernadsky, V. (1908/2002), "Academic life," in Vladimir Vernadsky, *On science*, 2, Saint Petersburg: Russian Christian Humanitarian Institute, pp. 168–176.

Vernadsky, V. (1911/2002), "Crush," in Vladimir Vernadsky, *On science*, Saint Petersburg: Russian Christian Humanitarian Institute, pp. 177–181.

Walteros, P. (2008), "La investigación en la actividad universitaria," *Areté*, 8, pp. 5–8.

Yin, R. K. (2003), *Case study research. Design and methods*, Thousand Oaks, CA: Sage.

Zeegers Paget, D., Barnhoorn, F., McCarthy, M., Alexanderson, K., Conceição, C., Devillé, W., Grimaud, O., Katreniakova, Z., Narkaustaité, L., Saliba, A., Sammut, M., and Voss, M. (2013), "Civil society engagement in innovation and research through the European Public Health Association," *Eur J Public Health*, 23 (Suppl. 2), pp. 12–18.

CHAPTER 5

# Case Study: Teaching and Research in Georgia

## 5.1. Introduction

In this chapter, we describe our experience of teaching and research in Georgia.[1] More specifically, we discuss how both teaching and research are organized and managed. The reason why we find it necessary to describe this is to understand, on the one hand, the challenges a university may face in the modern world and, on the other, to open a discussion on the possibilities of transforming classical approaches to education and research when they become products of mass consumption and excellence. From this perspective, we believe that the ways of administering and developing Georgian universities offer an interesting opportunity to understand not only the present state of university life but also to imagine its near future.

The topics we aim to cover in this chapter include both academic and non-academic aspects. Academic topics will include the accreditation of university programs, the organization of university libraries and university presses, difficulties related to the publication of research data, and the professional qualifications of university administrators. Non-academic topics will cover the management of teaching and research, as well as the intra-institutional respect between administrative and academic staff.

## 5.2. Academic Topics

Among the many difficulties that academic staff in Georgia may experience, a primary issue is professional disrespect and being ignored, especially regarding their exclusion from faculty governance. Most universities in our country, both public and private, are governed by a small number of academic and administrative staff who form an elite group that makes all decisions within the university, from the number and color of benches in the yard to the components of the curriculum. Despite their professional qualifications, this privileged segment of the university society elaborates and monitors the implementation of teaching and research plans in all sciences, determines the development paths of the university, including international cooperation, announces calls for research grants, and establishes salaries, both fixed and hour-based. Unfortunately, in almost all cases, the academic staff lacks the will to protest against non-professional decisions made by this minority. Rather, they obey silently and prefer not to protest loudly, as the golden rule of Georgian universities dictates: there are no academicians who cannot be fired, regardless of their professional teaching and research merits. As Carlos París has noted, for the real university to configure its features in approximation to the ideal described in the previous chapter, the support of the administration and society is necessary, but above all, those of us who work and study in this institution must feel like protagonists and responsible for an irreplaceable common effort. The university community is going through a period of demoralization that is affecting all of us in very different ways.[2]

Another way of silencing professors is the tendency of university administration to evaluate the quality of professors based on student evaluations. At the end of the semester or academic year, students fill out an anonymous questionnaire that assesses their satisfaction with the program and the teacher: how clear the professor was, and their impression of the professor's professional qualifications. There have been cases where students who failed at the end of the academic year wrote negative evaluations of professors, resulting in the non-renewal of their contracts at the beginning of the new academic year. This has led to self-censorship among professors, who, fearing negative evaluations, tend to give better marks to students during midterms and final examinations.

There are no tenure contracts at Georgian universities. Some offer contracts for 3, 5, or 7 years, but even in these cases, the contracts must be renewed annually. There is no guarantee of job stability, and even a fixed monthly salary for classes already delivered may easily be annulled if the university administration is dissatisfied with a particular professor.

What can be deduced from this secondary position of academicians is that the generation of new ideas within academia is a rare phenomenon. Naturally, members of the university elite "know" better what to research and how to teach in all fields of science, but still, the monotony of teaching and research life culminates in low productivity compared to foreign institutions.

One major difficulty that professors at Georgian universities may face during their contracts is a significant deficiency of specialized literature. Books in the contemporary world are expensive, and academic books are even more so. To carry out a research project and write a draft paper, it is always necessary to acquire new books, and not just a few, but a substantial number of recently published monographs. In Western European countries, where the authors of this book have had the opportunity to teach and conduct research, special funds are allocated for purchasing books, which are then moved to the university library at the end of the project. However, this is not the case in Georgia. We have experienced significant difficulty with university administrations when applying for lists of textbooks and monographs for purchase. The number of books in the lists was often reduced, and those that were ordered arrived with significant delays. The common argument from administrative staff is that universities have access to databases and that books can be retrieved from there. However, this is not true. First, most books, especially recently published ones, are not digitized because publishing is a business; second, Georgian universities do not have full access to databases because it is quite expensive to pay for this access. Another argument from the administration is that there is little need to buy full access as researchers in Georgia seldom use the databases. In summary, this creates a vicious cycle that reinforces itself with detrimental results.

We recall one case from our experience: one private university asked us to deliver lectures on "Research Methodology in Biomedical Sciences" during a semester. Following standard practice, we sent a request to the dean's office asking for the syllabus. We received a several-page document describing the 12 topics covered by 5 lecturers. It appeared to be a copy-and-paste version of the content of several books on "Research Methodology": the topics were not organized following a classical scheme of theoretical and practical approaches to research, such as first discussing the philosophy of social and biomedical sciences, followed by specific research instruments used in biomedical research; some questions from Molecular Biology were included, others were ignored. But what surprised us most was the section describing mandatory and secondary literature for the course. In the mandatory literature section, the word "Reader" was written—a single word without any description of the reader, who composed it, or which sources were used. When we asked at the university library, we found that the mentioned "Reader" did not exist at all. But that was only one side of the problem. In the secondary literature section of the syllabus, it was stated: "<www.pubmed.com> (research database)." Not books and companions, nor articles, just the database.

Another difficulty is the process of program accreditation and institutional authorization that Georgian universities must pass regularly. The process is regulated by the Ministry of Education and Science of Georgia. The board of experts is composed of professors from Georgian universities, with one international expert heading it. The regulations are mostly formal by nature: Are there books in the library catalog? Does the university have the necessary laboratories

CHAPTER 5

for conducting experiments? In which room? However, nobody asks what sort of books are located on the shelves—we remember one case when a majority of books were donated by US citizens to a private Georgian university, including books on cooking, detective stories, etc. Regarding the laboratories, nobody checks what sort of experiments are planned according to the teaching curriculum and if their descriptions correlate positively with the existing lab equipment. The monitoring is very formal, and almost all universities in Georgia receive approval for the programs they present.

Planning and implementation of teaching programs also deserve discussion. If we observe the catalogs of courses and programs at private universities, we see that any novelty appearing at one university is soon replicated by another. For instance, programs in cinematography or musical education appeared in the Georgian education market almost simultaneously. However, the quality of these teaching programs is very low compared to their European counterparts and is mostly adjusted to the requirements of Georgian accreditation rather than teaching outcomes.

Private universities in Georgia are more prestigious compared to state ones, even though the situation may favor state universities in some research directions. The problem with private universities is that their founders, mostly businessmen who have invested in education due to increased demand from international students, particularly in the field of medicine, consider education to be purely a business and research merely a decoration. Most universities have founded so-called scientific journals, including as many foreign professors, mostly emeritus, in their editorial boards as possible, who do not directly participate in evaluating manuscripts. By promoting their own journals, universities try to create an illusion of being scientifically active, while publishing papers of their own MA and PhD students.

The administration of one private Georgian university purchased a very expensive confocal microscope produced by Zeiss a year before the COVID-19 pandemic. For the next three years, including two years due to the pandemic and the last year due to a lack of a technician, the microscope was not functioning. After this period, it became impossible to find qualified research staff to operate the microscope. Currently, one technician is invited to turn on the microscope and demonstrate it to students without any infrastructural and academic possibilities to use it in research. This case demonstrates that financial funds cannot contribute to research without adequate human resources. As Bernardo A. Houssay correctly noted, research depends on people and their qualifications, not on nice buildings and expensive machines.[3] We also recall Santiago Ramón y Cajal's reflection that in 1923 Spain had well-organized laboratories where almost nothing new was produced. According to Ramón y Cajal, this was due to two reasons: it is not enough to call oneself a researcher to be a researcher, and discoveries are made by people, not by scientific techniques and rich libraries.[4]

Since 2010, several Georgian state universities have implemented a radical change in publishing. University committees assessing the quality of scientific work have developed a special system for estimating scientific productivity, requiring their research staff to publish papers in peer-reviewed journals indexed in Web of Science or Scopus. The system of changes was also applied to PhD studies; students were required to publish in prestigious journals and, in the case of Life Sciences, to be the first author of the publication. The number of papers required before PhD defense varies from one university to another, but typically 2 or 3 papers are needed. Curiously and sometimes ridiculously, PhD supervisors often do not have publications in the journals their PhD students are asked to publish in. To avoid difficulties related to publications, especially in Medicine, most universities have accepted a regulation allowing publication in journals with a high impact factor. However, impact factors change over time, and it is not specified that the impact factor should be calculated over the last 3 or 5 years. Additionally, many journals in third countries charge high fees for publication and publish any text after a 24-hour review. There have been cases where the PDF of a published paper disappeared from the journal's website after some time. These difficulties have caused tensions within universities, as observed in one case where a PhD student's husband had a conflict in the dean's office. At that time, there were 52 PhD students at a very small medical faculty, and the majority did not manage to finish their doctoral studies. At another private Georgian university, we personally know two heads of medical departments who have been PhD candidates for the last 8 years.

One fact is worth noting here. University committees that formulate rules for publication and evaluate the scientific output of researchers are composed of administrative staff with no experience in publishing. These are young people, and for most of them, working in quality culture committees and committees on research and innovation is their first job experience. We recall one case when we submitted our monograph, published by Peter Lang International Academic Publishing Group, for financial remuneration. The university administration's reaction was surprising: we received an official letter stating that financial remuneration is issued only for publication in journals indexed in Scopus, and the "journal Peter Lang," as stated in the letter, was not indexed. Our young colleague from the research committee could not distinguish between a journal and a publishing house. To clarify the situation, we sent an explanatory email indicating that we were speaking about the publication of a book, not a paper, and that it was published as part of a book series, not in a journal. We also sent the webpage of the editorial rankings, pointing out that Peter Lang is a prestigious publisher. After weeks of silence, we finally received financial remuneration and an official document prepared by the financial department and signed by the rector, stating that the premium was issued due to the publication "in the journal Peter Lang."

As Georgian universities aim to improve their positions in international ranking systems that evaluate different components and achievements, their professors are asked to make their Google Scholar profiles as representative as possible. It was discovered that the deans of most private universities had no publications and could not manually fill their profiles. However, a solution was soon found: they added other researchers' publications to their profiles, and Google Scholar now shows that they have a certain number of citations. Scopus author profiles cannot be individually managed, explaining why deans do not have pages in Scopus.

One interesting fact was observed during a grant application by our colleague, a university professor, who needed to present the dean's documents to a scientific foundation. It was discovered that the appointed, and not selected, dean had not even completed a master's degree and, naturally, did not have a doctorate either.

To facilitate research in the country, the Georgian government founded the Rustaveli Foundation, a state-financed organization that issues grants and subsidies for conducting research. Two interesting observations can be derived from monitoring the foundation's annual reports: 1. Most of the grants are received by the same research groups, and 2. The sums reflected in the foundation's reports are never enough for conducting modern research. For example, the sums allocated for publishing are less than what is needed to publish a paper in a modern journal of biomedical studies. The only possible conclusion is that the grants serve as an additional salary for researchers, far from enough for conducting research and publishing papers.

Georgian universities do not offer separate contracts for research professors; all contracts include a workload for classes, and research is the last component considered when preparing and signing them. As the number of international students increases year by year, Georgian universities prefer to hire teaching, rather than research, professors. This approach does not stimulate research at the university level. In the early 20th century, Bernardo A. Houssay noted that when university administration discovers that some of its professors are conducting original research, they should be offered research professorships, positions that allow full dedication to investigation and reduction of class overload.[5]

Georgian universities do not recognize the importance of a sabbatical year. Research professors are not allowed to take an academic year off from teaching, nor are they encouraged to spend a whole year at research centers abroad to establish professional networks or write a book. Despite the fact that some universities theoretically admit the possibility of a sabbatical year, it is never practically realized.

Publishing is another difficulty among Georgian academic circles. Most professors at Georgian universities, especially in the social sciences, publish monographs locally, in publishing houses that are not peer-reviewed and do not perform any expertise of the submitted texts. As one historian declared to the authors of this book, Georgian history is more interesting to Georgians, and there is no need to publish it in international publishing houses. Naturally, this is not true; the history of any country is equally interesting to the whole academic community, despite its geographic borders or political system. We also recall a conversation with a philosophy professor who indicated that for her monograph (a short book of approximately 70 pages), she wrote an evaluation and sent it to another professor just to sign. She was very sad that nobody was interested in reading her short work.

Observing the websites of Georgian universities, one can find professors with 300, 400, or 500 publications, including 50 or more monographs in the fields of history, literature, or philosophy. It is very difficult to imagine how many hours a researcher would need to work each week to achieve such results. Naturally, most of these papers are published in non-peer-reviewed journals, and books appear in small, national-based publishing houses, most of which lack an index. The bibliographies are either composed of Georgian sources or enriched with a large number of English-language sources, added to create an academic impression. We recall the words of Bernardo A. Houssay noting that the quality of a professor's work should be assessed based on the originality and importance of their scientific work and the work done by their disciples, not based on oratory skills, years spent at the university, or the number of publications lacking true originality.[6]

Another difficulty in the publication process is the duration and quality of the peer-review process, which determines the average time of publishing. Reviewing a paper is a complex process for several reasons: 1. Reviewers are mostly unpaid, which does not accelerate the revision and upload of reviews to the journal website; 2. In most scientific fields, more than 80 percent of manuscripts are reviewed within 6 months, "with 2.03 review rounds before publication. In addition to this, authors take time to revise their work. On average, it takes 39 days to submit a revised version, and 92% of resubmissions are done within 3 months (99% in Public health, 79% in Economics and Business)."[7] Thus, converting a manuscript into a paper, that is, the appearance of its final version as a paper in a journal or a book chapter in a monograph, can take from one to several years if published by a high-standard, peer-reviewed publishing house. Naturally, it is impossible to publish several hundred papers following this scheme over a couple of decades, as seen in the publication lists of many Georgian researchers, especially in the social sciences.

Another peculiarity is in the field of biomedical studies, where a large number of authored papers is determined by co-authorship. Different types of scientific misconduct, such as gift authorship, authorship by coercion, or unsolicited authorship, make it possible to achieve 10, 20, or more publications per year. Georgian medical doctors, especially those on the academic staff of medical universities or biomedical research institutions, supervise many PhD dissertations (one supervisor may direct up to 10 PhD projects simultaneously) and are automatically listed as co-authors on each publication resulting from the PhD thesis.

All of the above demonstrates the weakness of scientific thought, a sort of mental impotence regarding the values and ethics of teaching and research in Georgia.

We recall the lines written by Bill Readings regarding the self-finding of an individual as a grand narrative of university function. Despite being written more than 25 years ago, these lines are still relevant: "So how are we to think the institution of the University in which we find ourselves? It is clear that in the University we can never "find ourselves," come into our birthright; we cannot achieve the pure auto-affection that brings thought to an end in the virtual presence of an entirely self-knowing and autonomous subject. Yet such a notion of self-finding has been, throughout the modern age, the grand narrative of the function of the University. The subject of human history strives for autonomy, for the self-knowledge that will free it from the chains of the past, from its debts to a nature and to a language that are not of its own making. Thus, Kant thought we could find ourselves as entirely reasonable. The German Idealists thought we could find ourselves as an ethnic culture. The technologies of today think we can find ourselves as "most excellent," to cite *Bill and Ted's Excellent Adventure*—a film that is an interesting attempt to understand the impossibility of historical thought once knowledge has itself become commodified as information."[8]

From our perspective, the only way to find, define, and realize ourselves is through an ethical approach; only an ethical approach to personality, individuality, and humanity may culminate in the creation of a university with function, idea, and intention.

## 5.3. Non-Academic Topics

Academic difficulties are only part of the problems observed within the Georgian university system. Another significant set of obstacles that complicate academic engagement involves non-academic, administrative issues that, despite their nature, are crucial for creating a collegial atmosphere within academia. Below, we discuss some of these issues, based on our experiences working at several Georgian universities.

One regrettable experience observed by the authors is the implementation of so-called e-journals for registering classes. These e-journals are part of university websites that are often poorly managed and prone to delays. At the beginning of each class, lecturers must turn on computers, open the journal, and record the start time; at the end, they must again record the end time. If the time interval is not indicated correctly, class hours are deducted from the lecturer's monthly salary. Due to frequent malfunctions of electronic systems and unreliable internet services, lecturers are stressed about correctly recording class times, resulting in wasted class time and subpar teaching. University administrations justify this monitoring by citing frequent instances of missed lectures by lecturers, which does not excuse the administration's totalitarian control over academic staff. Even if some lecturers are not responsible professionals, it does not justify imposing collective responsibility for the non-academic behavior of a few. This punitive system results in irritated lecturers, defective classes, and a total loss of mutual respect between academic and administrative staff.

Additional issues with e-journals include their restriction to specific classrooms as per the class schedule. If a class is held in a different room, the e-journal cannot be accessed on that computer. There have been instances where classrooms lacked computers because they were taken for repairs or used in meetings or conferences. In such cases, lecturers must email a colleague in the study department from their mobile or personal computer (if available) to explain why they cannot launch the e-journal, consuming extra class time.

Around ten years ago, before the e-journal system, lecturers at one public university in Georgia were monitored by students. A group of students, working as interns in various university departments, was asked by the newly appointed dean to patrol the corridors, check classrooms, and verify if classes were in session. These students, armed with lists of classroom numbers and lecturer names, would note absences and report to the dean. This practice was highly unethical, as it normalized class absenteeism and created a culture of student surveillance over lecturers' duties and responsibilities.

Administrative staff also face strict monitoring by university top management. Each department is equipped with electronic chips distributed among staff members. To enter their workspace, staff must scan their chips at electronic turnstiles, recording their arrival time. The same procedure applies when leaving. This system erodes trust and collegiality within Georgian universities.

These examples highlight a lack of ethical attitudes in the modern academic society. Even if these practices are unique to Georgia, they are noteworthy as modern educational phenomena. Human nature is consistent across countries and eras, and any deviation in one educational paradigm can easily manifest in another.

Infrastructural challenges also contribute to the discomfort. For instance, lecturers often do not know which part of the city their classes will be held in until a week before they start. To save money, universities do not build campus systems like those in Western Europe; instead, they rent or occasionally buy buildings or floors in existing structures, many of which require renovation: missing doors or windows, lacking ventilation systems in spring or summer, and heating systems in winter. Once, we had a lecture in one building and, with a 30-minute interval, a seminar in another several kilometers away. The web system notified lecturers of the location change, but students were informed that seminars would be in the same building. Consequently, we arrived late due to peak hour traffic, only to discover that students were waiting at a different building.

Another type of infrastructural challenge in Georgian universities is the lack of adequate working space. Most institutions do not provide designated areas for affiliated academic staff, and there are no resting or working spaces for visiting staff. Program supervisors and academic staff with administrative roles often share their offices with other staff from different administrative units. These rooms may lack proper windows or have non-functional ones, suffer from poor illumination, and lack table lamps for working in the evening.

Despite these infrastructural difficulties, many Georgian universities contractually require academic staff to spend hours on campus beyond their teaching and research duties. Attempts to clarify the rationale behind this regulation with the human resources department and the dean's office yielded only the response that it was a contractual obligation. This situation gives the impression that professors are treated more like decorative fixtures, expected to occupy the buildings during specified hours.

Moreover, the requirement for extra hours on campus extends beyond academic staff to include deans, vice-deans, department heads, and their members. These individuals are frequently overloaded with work, expected to remain at their workplaces beyond their official working hours without additional compensation. The lack of time-management skills among university administrators exacerbates this issue.

Foreign professionals face challenges as well. In one instance, a private university's dean of the School of Health Sciences refused to sign a contract with a biochemistry professor from Iran, citing a preference for hiring Georgian professors.

The practice of "imported semesters" adds another layer of complexity. Many Georgian universities with international medical students start semesters with one group and, a few weeks later, begin classes for another group. Lecturers initially deliver classes to the first group, then repeat the same topics for the new arrivals. There have been cases where newly arrived students were combined with existing groups, causing them to miss initial lectures. This was attributed to a lack of classroom space.

The COVID-19 pandemic prompted Georgian universities to adopt online platforms for delivering classes. Sometimes classes were live, while other times they were recorded and uploaded for students. Post-pandemic, some universities continued using recorded classes for new international students without informing lecturers, including these classes in their workload, or compensating them.

A particular incident highlights the infrastructural inadequacies. After moving to a newly renovated building, lecturers found that the heating system was incomplete, forcing them to teach in coats during October and November. The WIFI system was non-functional, hindering the demonstration of online resources, and the cafeteria was closed, leaving students without access to drinking water. Despite promises that renovations would soon be complete, classes continued under these conditions.

University cafeterias also present issues. They often open late, close early, or remain shut on Saturdays due to low student turnout, making it inconvenient for staff and students. Libraries follow similar patterns, with restricted hours, especially during vacations and examination periods.

Laboratory classes face significant challenges as well. In one histology class, a laboratory initially equipped with 10 microscopes accommodated 14 students. As three microscopes broke down (they were manufactured in China and were of low quality. Zeiss microscopes, for instance, are more expensive, the fact resulting decisive for university administration to buy cheaper Chinese analogs), the group size increased to 18 students (4 students were included in the group in the middle of the semester), yet the administration refused to split the group to avoid paying for extra seminar hours.

A private university's move to a new building labeled various rooms as specialized laboratories (Maternal and child health simulation laboratory, First aid simulation laboratory, High technology simulation laboratory, Physiology laboratory, Human anatomy laboratory, or Histology laboratory) but the equipment remained the same: basic desks and projectors without distinguishing features. All minimal laboratorial equipment including electronic scales and 10 microscopes (monocular) were gathered on the third floor. Lecturers in histology had to manually transport microscopes between floors each time they have classes.

Furthermore, universities generate additional revenue by charging staff for parking and offering expensive cafeteria services without discounts for students or professors. There are no cards or reduced prices for students and professors.

The issues discussed here represent only a fraction of the academic and non-academic challenges in Georgian universities. Each semester brings new problems, underscoring the devaluation of basic educational values. These experiences are significant culturally and may offer valuable insights when compared with practices in other countries, illustrating different expectations of university life. As Hannah Arendt noted, "It is somewhat difficult to take a crisis in education as seriously as it deserves. It is tempting indeed to regard it as a local phenomenon, unconnected with the larger issues of the century."[9]

## Notes

1. Some recent publications discuss Georgian universities, such as Tavadze, 2023, 2024; Oleksiyenko, 2023; Oleksiyenko and Tavadze, 2024; Kobakhidze and Samniashvili, 2022.
2. París, 1983, pp. 10–11.
3. Houssay, 1939, p. 22.
4. Ramón y Cajal, 1952, p. 102.
5. Houssay, 1939, p. 24.
6. Ibid., p. 18.
7. Rodriguez Medina, 2020, pp. 1–2.
8. Readings, 1999, pp. 52–53.
9. Arendt cited in Pelikan, 1992, p. 13.

## Bibliography

Houssay, B. (1939), "Recuerdos de un professor y consideraciones sobre la investigación," in Marota P., *El Profesor Bernanrdo A. Houssay (Discursos pronunciados con motive de su designación como profesor honorario)*, Buenos Aires: Imprenta Universidad de Buenos Aires, pp. 11–27.

Kobakhidze, N., and Samniashvili, L. (2022), "Less USSR, more democracy please!": Hope and discontent in Georgia's quest for academic freedom," *Higher Education Quarterly*, 76(3), pp. 595–611.

Oleksiyenko, A. (2023), "De-Sovietisation of Georgian higher education: deconstructing unfreedom," *Quality in Higher Education*, 29(1), pp. 6–22.

Oleksiyenko, A. and Tavadze, G. (2024), "Decolonization of post-Soviet higher education: critical inquiry through a reflexive scholarly dialogue," *Cultural Studies ↔ Critical Methodologies*, pp. 1–12.

París, C. (1983), *Lección inaugural del curso académico 1983–1984*, Madrid: Ciudad Universitaria de Cantoblanco.

Pelikan, J. (1992), *The idea of the university. A reexamination*, New Haven and London: Yale University Press.

Ramón y Cajal, S. (1952), *Los tónicos de la voluntad: Reglas y consejos sobre investigación científica*, Buenos Aires: Espasa-Calpe.

Readings, B. (1999), *The university in ruins*, Cambridge, MA: Harvard University Press.

Rodriguez Medina, L. (2020), "On urgency and importance," *Tapuya: Latin American Science, Technology and Society*, 3:1, pp. 1–3.

Tavadze, G. (2023), "From the thin concept of quality to the thick one: Remedial responsibilities of the universities," *Quality in Higher Education*, 29(1), pp. 102–115.

Tavadze, G. (2024), "The post-Soviet scholar: from the spaces of inaction towards public thinking and multiple agoras," in Gibbs, P., de Rijke, V., Peterson, A. (eds.), *The contemporary scholar in higher education*, Cham: Palgrave Macmillan, pp. 173–191.

CHAPTER 6

# Human Happiness

## 6.1. Introduction

The first attempts to define and characterize the notion of "happiness" were made by ancient Greek philosophers. They described it as the highest good and taught Hedonism as an ethical doctrine at different philosophical schools, such as the Cyrenaics and Epicureans. From a psychological point of view, "happiness" was explained and defined as "pleasure." Plato described *pleasure* as a replenishment, noting that some types of pleasure are pure and unmixed by nature, different from *knowledge*. Aristotle defined "happiness" as a higher or better good compared to other sorts of goods. For him, *pleasure* was an experience that accompanies unimpeded activity. Augustine considered *pleasure* a kind of passion linked to the *will*. Aquinas defined pleasure as the "arrest" of desire for a loved object.[1]

The ideas cultivated in the ancient world were later discussed and enriched by Western philosophers. From a historical perspective, the views of Jeremy Bentham, John Stuart Mill, and David Hume are of major importance.

According to Jeremy Bentham, there is a direct relation between action and its results. In other words, the right action is the one that produces the most happiness. Bentham considered happiness a product of individual perception, observing a certain correlation between *pleasure* and *pain*. People seek *pleasures* and try to avoid *pain*, noted Bentham, who attempted to calculate *happiness* by its duration and intensity, and its potential to lead to other *pleasures*. Once we subtract the elements of *pain*, Bentham argued, pure *happiness* is left. However, Bentham's equal treatment of all *pleasures* resulted in critical acceptance. Bentham's view that all ways of bringing the same amount of *pleasure* should be valued equally was further developed by John Stuart Mill.[2]

John Stuart Mill considered it necessary to differentiate types of *pleasure* and to regard some as better than others. For instance, according to Mill, the *lower pleasures* experienced by animals cannot be compared to the highly intellectual ones experienced by humans. Despite the convincing nature of Mill's argument, he was criticized for the impossibility of measuring different qualities of *happiness*, as some are higher and others lower.[3]

David Hume authored four essays in which he described different ideas regarding human life and *happiness*. The first essay, "The Epicurean," focuses on natural pleasures and denies the possibility of creating artificial ones. In the second, "The Stoic," Epicurean hedonism is replaced by the importance of *art* and *industry* in building human happiness. The third, "The Platonist," features the philosopher as a man of contemplation, while the fourth, "The Sceptic," focuses not on the particular object of *happiness* but on "the passion itself."[4]

In this book, we are interested in *happiness* from an educational perspective. In other words, we aim to explore how education can lead to a *sense of pleasure*. This feeling would be similar to other sorts of *pleasure* and, at the same time, different, as it can only be achieved through education.[5]

## 6.2. University and Human Happiness

First, we should try to define what we understand as being educated. Here lies an approximation to the notion of education, on the one hand, and the feeling of being educated, on the other. Education, as the cultivation of character and a state balanced by ethics and responsibility, is a subject of investigation in various disciplines such as general psychology, clinical psychology, philosophy, cultural studies, law, and many others. Education, as a feeling discovered by an individual and perceived as *pleasure*, is a subjective perception that varies from person to person and philosopher to philosopher. Both sides of it—as an ethical character and as subjective self-encounter—coexist and complicate the differentiation or continuation of one side into the other. From some points of view, this sort of pleasure may be *fictional*. We shall discuss the fictional nature of education below.

It is observed that meeting and conversing with an educated individual is accompanied by a certain sense of *pleasure*. Regardless of the topic of conversation and its length, we note that time flies, and we regret that the conversation eventually comes to an end. Once remembered, we seek similar contexts to exchange ideas and communicate our feelings and dreams. The gap between boredom and joy is bridged, and our brain starts experiencing *pleasure*.

But what is the reason for this? Why do we find talking with educated people attractive and find ourselves lost in conversation with others? Naturally, we do not realize that the basic idea of feeling happy is linked to the years our interlocutor spent in libraries. The feeling we perceive as *happiness* is, above all, in the moment of the conversation and can only be compared with other strong and long-lasting feelings, like love, hate, or memories.

In his famous book *A Little History of Philosophy*, Nigel Warburton, in a chapter on Jeremy Bentham, discusses the possibilities of measuring *happiness* by linking it with personal memories. Warburton recalls a trip on a water taxi in Venice with his wife and children, with the beautiful view, the sunset, and the laughter of his family.[6] Naturally, we cannot measure *happiness* empirically, but it can be kept or prolonged in time once it finds a place in our memories. However, the intensity of feelings as part of memory will not be similar to that experienced in the concrete context, in the very moment of acting.

*Happiness* may be felt and encountered in different places, among which the university is one of the most frequent and natural. Frequent, as the university is a hub of educated individuals, and natural, as the transmission and dissemination of new knowledge is a university function. People do not keep knowledge to themselves; rather, they are oriented to share it. What brings the sense of *happiness* is not only the process of acquiring knowledge but also the process of sharing it. A lecture successfully delivered, an experiment successfully conducted, or a paper published in a journal represents a source of *happiness* that is communicable, like an infectious disease. Just as microorganisms need hosts for development, we need an audience to share our ideas and achievements to be happy.

The audience is a space in which university professionals are self-realized. A higher level of education determines a greater variety of feelings achieved and perceived as happy feelings. This is an environment in which everyone is happy—the degree may vary, but the feeling will persist. Over time, we become increasingly attracted to the idea of doing something that can make other people happy. Gradually, this transforms into a custom, allowing people to create new and diverse contexts for their better self-realization.

In his essay on education, James Mill noted that the end of education "is to render the individual […] an instrument of happiness, first to himself, and next to other beings. The properties, by which he is fitted to become an instrument to this end, are, partly, those of the body, and partly those of the mind."[7] Indeed, the way to happiness is not a blind alley; rather, it is a communicative space that ensures the movement of energy within the channels of human communication. People experience happiness in company, sharing feelings and ideas, and receiving immediate feedback on what they share. One cannot be active today and happy tomorrow. Happiness is perceived in the process of acting, as soon as it starts, and it is over once the act is realized. Our brain remembers the experienced feeling and tries to create new behavioral schemes that may result in the reappearance of similar situations leading to similar perceptions.

Now we should rethink the idea of the *fictional* nature of education mentioned earlier. Despite being based on factual knowledge, the very structure of this basis is imagined by each individual. There are general teaching plans for professions, but each individual creates a personal approach to it. This may be called specialization in learning and later in professional acting. The directions our studies shape, the paths our teaching follows, and the degree to which our happiness is felt are all individual. This individuality is imagined; it is fictional, as we cannot realize it in any other way, modeled on the behavior and professional life of others. That is why education, or how we build our character, both professional and spiritual, is a product of our fiction, our imagination, and is subject to changes according to the metamorphoses of the contexts in which we live and self-realize.

Universities are ideal spaces for experiencing human happiness. Students offer a rich source for generating new teaching and research ideas: they ask new questions, propose different solutions, and create new connections within existing teaching frameworks. The integration of new ideas into the formation of educational trends is a highly productive process. Lecturers analyze these new approaches based on their expertise, and the symbiosis between students and teachers leads to educational advances. Happiness is created in the moment of these advances. Pleasure is felt in understanding one's possibilities. Collaboration between minds leads to mutual respect and a sense of professional and human friendship. This is frequently observed in academia, where colleagues often become close friends over time.

One very illustrative example of successful collaboration within academia is the so-called "scientific school." A professor,[8] or sometimes a group of investigators,[9] serves as the generator of ideas that are later developed in the works of their disciples. This is how ideas continue through time, evolving in the works of new generations of researchers. Sometimes the ideas are slightly modified from their original form; other times, the changes are more significant, or the ideas transform into entirely new thoughts.[10] In all cases, the process of creation, interpretation, analysis, transformation, disappearance, or reappearance of ideas is a context in which happiness is realized and achieved.

Scientific schools can also be based on the development of disciplines, as was the case with the development of Rhetoric in the 20th century. This includes the context of New Rhetoric,[11] within which developed the Rhetoric of Argumentation, which places the argumentative structure of discourse at the center of its study,[12] Structuralist Rhetoric,[13] and General Textual Rhetoric,[14] proposed by Antonio García Berrio. The latter formed a basis for the development of Cultural Rhetoric.[15]

At this stage of university development, when scientific schools are created and disciples develop the ideas of their teachers, the individual possibilities of researchers become crucial for creating human happiness. The notion of "individuality" reappears and invites us to reflect further on the importance of human potential. In his famous text *On Liberty*, John Stuart Mill discusses the role of individuality in the self-realization of a free person.[16] Mill contrasts human potential with the ape-like mode of imitation, emphasizing the importance of personal decisions in action. Distinguishing humans from machines built after a model, Mill considers it necessary to include elements of spontaneity and individuality in choosing one's plan of life. The importance of the questions discussed by Mill is especially evident in times of crisis, as seen during the COVID-19 pandemic.[17]

However, individuality alone is not enough to stimulate education and research. Ideas are generated by individuals, but their cultivation, discussion, and interpretation are realized by groups of colleagues, disciples, and students. Collaboration in academia is essential for advances in university life. Collaboration is of major importance for the successful development of ideas. International collaboration forms a solid foundation for the exchange of ideas cultivated in different cultural epistemes and leads to joint publications that facilitate better dissemination of scientific ideas. From this perspective, teamwork and collaboration create spaces that foster human happiness.

To achieve the necessary collaboration in academia, collegial relationships based on mutual respect are essential. Academic success results from trust and friendship among colleagues and students. University administrations should trust and respect lecturers, and lecturers should share their knowledge and experience with students. This is possible in a society where ethics rule, with the sole aim of making those around us happier. This cannot be achieved in a society where excellence is the only goal, measured by various web portals' metrics for publications and citations. It cannot be achieved through competition between universities and research groups, with strict deadlines and turning education into a pure business. If the goal of academia is to enrich administrative personnel by turning lecturers into mere hired hands, the system will fail because a university is not a farm. People are not machines. Delivering twenty hours of classes per week leaves no space for research or friendly communication between colleagues. In such circumstances, everyone will try to work less, lower the quality of classes, and avoid professional responsibility. In such an atmosphere, students will be less interested in their studies. They will not see the connection between university years and their future profession. University life will become a business enterprise. Universities print diplomas, and students pay to receive them. There will be no space for building individual character, creating new possibilities, and expanding horizons. If universities continue to develop in this direction, things will worsen, and human happiness may be irreversibly lost within the universities. This is the problem of modern academia, and it seems almost impossible to solve it in the near future.

## Notes

1. Brennan, 1973.
2. Burns, 2005; Warburton 2011, pp. 121–125.
3. Nussbaum, 2005; Warburton 2011, pp. 138–144.
4. Immerwahr, 1989.
5. On the pursuit of happiness, see Narens and Skyrms, 2020; on happiness and universities, see Gibbs, 2017.
6. Warburton 2011, pp. 122–123.
7. Mill, 1992, p. 137.
8. As in case of Tartu-Moscow Semiotic School, led by Juri Lotman and studying the questions of semiotics of culture.
9. As in case of Birmingham School of Cultural Studies or Birmingham School of Economics.
10. On this topic see approaches to *interdiscursivity* (Gómez-Moriana, 1997; Albaladejo, 2005, 2007, 2008, 2012; Albaladejo and Chico Rico, 2022; Luarsabishvili, 2018; Rodríguez Pequeño, 2020), *intertextuality* (Kristeva, 1967, 1974; Martínez Fernández, 2001; Martín Jiménez, 2015; Gómez Alonso, 2017), and *interideity* (Luarsabishvili, 2022).
11. Pozuelo Yvancos, 1988; Chico Rico, 2015.
12. Perelman and Olbrechts-Tuteca, 1989.
13. Grupo μ, 1987.
14. García Berrio 1984, 2009.
15. Albaladejo, 2009, 2012, 2013, 2014, 2016, 2019a, 2019b, 2019c; Gallor Guarín, 2019; Luarsabishvili (ed.) 2023, Luarsabishvili, 2024.
16. Mill, 1992.
17. Kiladze and Luarsabishvili, 2024.

## Bibliography

Albaladejo, T. (2005), "Retórica, comunicación, interdiscursividad," *Revista de Investigación Lingüística* 8/1, pp. 7–34.

Albaladejo, T. (2007), "Semiótica, traducción literaria y análisis interdiscursivo," in Miguel Ángel Garrido Gallardo y Emilio Frechilla Díaz (eds.), *Teoría/Crítica. Homenaje a la Profesora Carmen Bobes Naves*, Madrid: Consejo Superior de Investigaciones Científicas, pp. 61–75.

Albaladejo, T. (2008), "Poética, Literatura Comparada y análisis interdiscursivo," *Acta Poética* 29/2, pp. 245–274.

Albaladejo, T. (2009), "La poliacroasis en la representación literaria: un componente de la Retórica Cultural," *Castilla. Estudios de Literatura*, 0, pp. 1–26.

Albaladejo, T. (2012), "Literatura comparada y clases de discursos. El análisis interdiscursivo: textos literarios y forales de Castilla y de Portugal," in R. Alemany Ferrer and F. Chico Rico (eds.), *Literatures ibèriques medievals comparades/Literaturas ibéricas medievales comparadas*, Alicante, Sociedad Española de Literatura general y Comparada: Universidad de Alicante, pp. 15–38.

Albaladejo, T. (2013),"Retórica cultural, lenguaje retórico y lenguaje literario," *Tonos Digital: Revista de estudios filológicos*, 25, pp. 1–21.

Albaladejo, T. (2014), "La Retórica cultural ante el discurso de Emilio Castelar," in Juan Carlos Gómez Alonso et al. (eds.), *Constitución republicana de 1873 autógrafa de D. Emilio Castelar*, Madrid: UAM Ediciones, pp. 293–319.

Albaladejo, T. (2016), "Cultural rhetoric. Foundations and perspectives," *Res Rhetorica*, III, 1, pp. 17–29.

Albaladejo, T. (2019a), "Retórica cultural y textualidad. A propósito de un discurso forense de Juan Meléndez Valdés," in Ramón González Ruiz, Inés Olza Moreno and Óscar Loureda Lamas (eds.), *Lengua, cultura, discurso. Estudios ofrecidos al profesor Manuel Casado Velarde*, Pamplona: Eunsa, pp. 83–98.

Albaladejo, T. (2019b), "Generación metafórica y redes semánticas en la poesía de Antonio Cabrera: En la estación perpetua," in Sergio Arlandis (ed.), *Contraluz de pensamiento. La poesía de Antonio Cabrera*, Sevilla: Renacimiento, pp. 160–195.

Albaladejo, T. (2019c), "El motor metafórico y la fundamentación retórico-cultural de su activación," *Castilla. Estudios de Literatura*, 10, pp. 559–583.

Albaladejo, T. and Chico Rico, F. (2022), "Retórica y Estudios del Discurso," in Carmen López Ferrero, Isolda E. Carranza, Teun A. van Dijk (eds.), *Estudios del discurso. The Routledge Handbook of Spanish Language Discourse Studies*, London and New York: Routledge, pp. 101–114.

Brennan, J. G. (1973), *Ethics and morals*, New York: Harper & Raw Publishers.

Burns, J. H. (2005), "Happiness and utility: Jeremy Bentham's equation," *Utilitas*,17(1), pp. 46–61.

Chico Rico, F. (2015), "La Retórica cultural en el contexto de la Neorretórica," *Dialogía. Revista de lingüística, literatura y cultura*, 9, pp. 304–322.

Gallor Guarín, J. O. (2019), *El Diálogo de doctrina christiana de Juan de Valdés. Retórica cultural, discurso y literatura*, Alicante: Departamento de Publicaciones de la Universidad de Alicante.

García Berrio, A. (1984), "Retórica como ciencia de la expresividad (Presupuestos para una Retórica General)," *Estudios de Lingüística Universidad de Alicante*, 2, pp. 7–59.

García Berrio, A. (2009), *El centro en lo múltiple (Selección de ensayos), II. El contenido de las formas (1985–2005)*, edition and introductory study by Enrique Baena, Barcelona: Anthropos.

Gibbs, P. (2017), *Why universities should seek happiness and contentment?*, London: Bloomsbury.

Gómez Alonso, J. C. (2017), "Intertextualidad, intediscursividad y Retórica Cultural," *Tropelías. Revista de Teoría de la Literatura y Literatura Comparada*, Número extraordinario 1 (Homenaje a José Enrique Martínez Fernández), pp. 107–115.

Gómez-Moriana, A. (1997), "Du texte au discours. Le concept d'*interdiscursivité*," *Versus*, 77–78, pp. 57–73.

Grupo μ (1987), *Retórica general*, Barcelona: Paidós.

Immerwahr, J. (1989), "Hume's essays on happiness," *Hume Studies*, 15 (2), pp. 307–324.

Kiladze, M. and Luarsabishvili, V. (2024), *The legitimization of violence. Individual, crowd and authority during the Covid-19 pandemic*, New York: Peter Lang.

Kristeva, J. (1967), "Bajtin, le mot, le dialogue et le roman," *Critique*, 239, pp. 438–465.

Kristeva, J. (1974), *El texto de la novela*, Barcelona: Lumen.

Luarsabishvili, V. (2018), "Análisis interdiscursivo, Retórica, Traducción e Intertextualidad," *Archivum*, LXVIII, pp. 93–114.

Luarsabishvili, V. (2022), *Teoría de la interideidad. Gustavo Adolfo Bécquer y Miguel de Unamuno*, Valladolid: Universidad de Valladolid.

Luarsabishvili, V. (ed.) (2023), *Cultural rhetoric. Rhetorical perspectives, transferential insights* (Book series *Rethinking society. individuals, culture and migration*, v. 4). Tbilisi: New Vision University Press.

Luarsabishvili, V. (2024), *Retórica cultural: metáfora, contexto, traducción. Las voces de Rubén Darío, Miguel de Unamuno, Gabriel Aresti, Kirmen Uribe y Harkaitz Cano*, Oxford: Peter Lang.

Martínez Fernández, J. E. (2001), *La intertextualidad literaria*, Madrid: Cátedra.

Martín Jiménez, A. (2015), "La imitación y el plagio en el Clasicismo y los conceptos contemporáneos de intertextualidad e hipertextualidad," *Dialogía. Revista de Lingüistica, Literatura y Cultura*, 9, pp. 58–100.

Mill, J. (1992), "Education," in Terence Ball (ed.), *James Mill, Political writings*, Cambridge: Cambridge University Press, pp. 137–194.

Mill, J. S. (1992), "On liberty," in John Stuart Mill (ed.), *On liberty and utilitarianism*, London: David Campbell Publishers.

Narens, L. and Skyrms, B. (2020), *The pursuit of happiness: philosophical and psychological foundations of utility*, Oxford: Oxford University Press.

Nussbaum, M. (2005), "Mill between Aristotle and Bentham," in Luigino Bruni and Pier Luigi Porta (eds.), *Economics and Happiness*, Oxford: Oxford University Press, pp. 170–183.

Perelman, C. and L. Olbrechts-Tyteca (1989), *Tratado de la argumentación. La nueva retórica*, Madrid: Gredos.

Pozuelo Yvancos, J. M. (1988), "Retórica general y Neorretórica", in José María Pozuelo Yvancos, *Del Formalismo a la Neorretórica*, Madrid: Taurus, pp. 181–211.

Rodríguez Pequeño, J. (2020), "Ficcionalidad e interdiscursividad: el arte de lenguaje en Joaquín Sabina," *Piedras Lunares*, 4, pp. 97–113.

Warburton, N. (2011), *A little history of philosophy*, New Heaven and London: Yale University Press.

CHAPTER 7

# Conclusions

The question of how to organize and administer universities has been a subject of discussion across different cultures and eras. Education, research, and social responsibility have been core topics of debate. The ethical component, evident in every aspect of university life, has been recognized as important and prominent. All these elements serve, and continue to serve, the self-realization of individuals, culminating in personal well-being and happiness. Therefore, it is not surprising to find the notion of "freedom" in various texts that describe and reflect on the idea of the university.

The freedom of individual scientists and scientific institutions is of major importance when discussing the idea of science, its nature, philosophy, and potential to improve our lives. Connected with the sense of responsibility, freedom is considered to be *responsible* freedom, distinct from arbitrariness.[1]

Education invites individuals into a new, unknown world; it opens doors to new impressions and offers possibilities for thinking that, in turn, develop imagination. Today's knowledge is detailed, multilayered, and accumulated from various sciences. It is transdisciplinary and creates an illusion of possession. We think we possess knowledge, can control it, and use it when necessary. But reality is different. In moments of crisis, when knowledge is needed most, we discover that what we have is only a small portion, insufficient for effective action. This was evident during the first year of the COVID-19 pandemic when we struggled to manage it and provide adequate professional medical assistance. Even before the pandemic, in 2015 and 2016, it was well-known that some coronaviruses posed potential dangers,[2] yet existing prototypes of SARS vaccines were ineffective.[3]

Is education an instrument? Are medical doctors true professionals or merely followers of guidelines without deeper analysis of medical cases? How deeply do medical professionals distinguish between *disease*, *illness*, *sickness*, and *malady* in practice?[4] Or is education a profession in itself? Can knowledge be transmitted from professor to student, or must it be acquired individually based on practical experience? What is the role of the teacher in offering and explaining the basics of a profession? What is the role of the student in teaching and learning? How effective can the institutionalization of education be? These and similar questions require deep reflection on the nature, goals, and potential outcomes of education. Naturally, these goals and results will vary across different epochs and contexts.

Teaching methods differ from generation to generation. Technological progress facilitates teaching planning and creates diverse perspectives on its implementation. E-learning was a step forward, and the creation of joint programs and degrees became an emerging necessity. The same applies to research: PhDs by publication represent a new approach to transforming both teaching and research, and joint publications and multiple institutional affiliations (double or triple) demonstrate the necessity of combining possibilities for better education and research.[5] Modern challenges in academic life will create new perspectives that will inevitably deepen both educational and research approaches.

To make all this possible, it is crucial to have staff dedicated to both teaching and research. Professors should be interested in research and not overloaded with classes to have enough time and resources (physical and emotional) for research. Their positions should be *full-time*, allowing them to concentrate on their work. They should be paid adequately to support their families and not need a second or third job. Their dedication to university life should be complete, fostering professional interests in both teaching and research. They must feel valued and see their classes, experiments, papers, and coordinated volumes appreciated by both their academic community and the wider society. Professors should be part of civic society, embodying noble qualities and serving as models of moral, cultural, and scientific excellence, as true teachers are carriers of eternal values.[6] Universities should not be isolated from society; they should be interconnected, forming professionals and individuals for all dimensions of life.[7] Only then can universities become attractive environments that create and share values for the well-being of society. Researchers possess proper judgment about the topics they teach and the capacity to stimulate and direct students' abilities. Researchers can maintain a passion for scientific studies over years of teaching, as their wide visions and structured knowledge inspire young generations.[8]

Research work in the modern world is a luxury not all countries can afford. Declaring a university as a *research* institution is insufficient; specific instruments are needed to measure the research output of groups, departments, or the entire university. It is better not to pursue research than to produce low-quality work published in local journals in minority languages. If new knowledge is not valid (concept validity, internal validity, and external validity), repeatable (the observation of the same results after repeating measurement), reproducible (taking into consideration, in the moment of planning a study, the factors that may cause variation), reliable, and widely shared, there is no point in wasting time and money. Instead, developing countries should translate and disseminate new knowledge produced in developed countries among students and professionals. Few countries are wealthy enough to conduct modern research with state-of-the-art laboratories and equipment. It is challenging to organize scientific work in developing countries.

However, having equipment is not enough for high-quality research. Professional qualifications are needed to operate microscopes and computers. Developing countries may struggle to educate teaching and research staff but can support their work by providing conditions for professional self-realization. If financial resources are lacking, there is no point in founding research institutions or scientific centers.

Beyond equipment and qualifications, the existence of investigational ideas based on professional scientific imagination is crucial. If universities lack colleagues to initiate and share new ideas, there is no research future. Universities cannot be closed, nation-based systems that do not invite foreign researchers for everyday collaboration. Short-term international visits are unproductive if researchers cannot continue international scientific conversations at home. All visits should culminate in tangible outcomes, such as joint publications.

University presses also play a vital role. Each university should have its own press to publish and disseminate new knowledge from its scientific community. However, there should be no restrictions on publishing elsewhere. Researchers should be encouraged to publish with international publishers like Routledge, CRC Press, Brill, Peter Lang, De Gruyter, and Springer to ensure their work reaches a global audience. Universities should also provide financial support for international publications, including copyediting and co-financing.

Technical equipment, repeated visits to foreign centers, and subsidies for publishing indicate the need for funds to support university development. Universities are either public or private. In Europe, public universities are more prestigious and better funded than private ones. In Asia, minimal progress in education and research is often achieved by private universities.

Measuring scientific output is challenging for both university administration and researchers. Publications in top-ranked journals are typically required, and citation indexes are used to measure productivity. However, citations accumulate quickly in Life Sciences but slowly in Humanities, and they do not fully reflect a work's impact. Auto-citations can inflate citation counts, and heads of

## CHAPTER 7

laboratories or scientific schools receive more citations than active researchers. Monographs in Humanities can be more productive as they offer more space for idea development, whereas Life Sciences papers are valued for their frequency. The peer-review process varies significantly between fields, making citations an unequal comparison tool.

Modern educational systems offer numerous grants and subsidies for studying abroad and enhancing qualifications. Programs like Erasmus and Horizon are productive for academic goals. However, upon returning, institutions must provide working conditions that match researchers' qualifications. Otherwise, years of acquired knowledge are wasted, leading to demotivation and career changes. Universities should avoid becoming mere offices, fostering productivity and excitement in academic life.

Today, university education is a mass-consumption product. Teaching has become a business, and attracting students, especially international ones, is financially driven, often at the expense of educational and research standards. In Eastern Europe and Asia, many universities attract students with easy registration, short and superficial programs, and minimal practical and research components. Professors are poorly paid and overworked, leading to a lack of motivation for research. As Bill Readings noted, "the University is no longer Humboldt's, and that means it is no longer *The University*. The Germans not only founded a university and gave it a mission; they also made the University into the decisive instance of intellectual activity."[9]

We hope that the situation regarding universities will improve. Academic staff will be more respected, and the responsibility toward students will increase. Students should actively understand the direct relation between their studies and future professions, helping to shape their wills, connect them with their professional vocation, and determine their well-being and happiness in both professional and private life.

## Notes

1. Mittelstrass, 2018, p. 151.
2. Vineet D. Menachery et al., 2015; Vineet D. Menachery et al., 2016.
3. MacKenzie, 2017.
4. One may not have read the dissertation of sociologist Andrew Twaddle which elaborated the mentioned distinction but understanding the nature of the listed notions will be helpful for better management of different changes (observable, measurable, examinable and emotional). On this topic, see Hofmann, 2017.

5. Hottenrott and Lawson, 2016, 2021; Hottenrott et al., 2020.
6. Pacheco Gómez, 1995, p. 55.
7. París, 1976: 70.
8. Houssay, 1939: 18.
9. Readings, 1999, p. 55.

## Bibliography

Hofmann, B. (2017), "Disease, illness, and sickness," in Miriam Solomon, Jeremy R. Simon, and Harold Kincaid (eds.), *The Routledge companion to philosophy of medicine*, New York and London: Routledge, pp. 16–26.

Hottenrott, H., Lawson, C. (2016), "A first look at multiple institutional affiliations: a study of authors in Germany, Japan and the UK," *Scientometrics*, 111, pp. 285–295.

Hottenrott, H., Rose, M. E., Lawson, C. (2020), "The rise of multiple institutional affiliations in academia," *J. Assoc. Inf. Sci. Technol.*, 72, pp. 1039–1058.

Hottenrott, H., Lawson, C. (2021), "What is behind multiple institutional affiliations in academia?," *Science and Public Policy*, 00, pp. 1–21.

Houssay, B. (1939), "Recuerdos de un profesor y consideraciones sobre la investigación," in Marota P., *El Profesor Bernardo A. Houssay (Discursos pronunciados con motivo de su designación como profesor honorario)*, Buenos Aires: Imprenta Universidad de Buenos Aires, pp. 11–27.

MacKenzie, D. (2017), "Plague! How to prepare for the next pandemic," *New Scientist*, February 22.

Mittelstrass, J. (2018), *Theoria: chapters in the philosophy of science*, Berlin: De Gruyter.

Pacheco Gómez, M. (1995), "Misión de la Universidad," *Anales de la Universidad de Chile*, 2, pp. 51–64.

París, C. (1976), *Ideas pedagógicas de B. Francisco Giner*, in *Centenario de la ILE*, Madrid: Tecnos.

Readings, B. (1999), *The university in ruins*, Cambridge, MA: Harvard University Press.

Vineet D. Menachery et al. (2015), "A SARS-like cluster of circulating bat coronaviruses shows potential for human emergence," *Nature Medicine*, 21, 12, pp. 1508–1513.

Vineet D. Menachery et al. (2016), "SARS-like WIV1-CoV poised for human emergence," *Proceedings of the National Academy of Sciences of the United States of America*, 113, 11, pp. 3048–3053.

# Postscript

The idea of writing this book was born from our practical experience in teaching and research. Having taught at different levels of university education in Georgia and abroad, and having published papers, monographs, and coordinated volumes with international publishing houses, we have reflected extensively and discussed the modern challenges faced by universities in our epoch. We have tried to compare our Georgian reality with international experiences, placing Georgian, German, Spanish, Swiss, and Latin American universities side by side as much as our experience and imagination allowed. Things are better understood in comparison, and we hope that our reflections will be productive and thought-provoking.

Probably "rethinking" is the correct word to describe our efforts in analyzing Georgian academic reality. Naturally, countries possess different traditions of thinking, teaching, and conducting research. There may not be universal approaches across different countries, or even within a single country or specific community. Approaches differ, and what makes them valuable is this difference. At the same time, education and research, as fundamental values on which the university community is based and self-realized, also differ from community to community. Cultural differences of societies that found and administer universities are evident in organizing teaching and research. All the aforementioned demands a multiple and transdisciplinary approach to our investigation, allowing for the formulation of interesting conclusions.

The devaluation of the nature of any single thing occurs as soon as it is converted into a product of mass consumption. In her text regarding the crisis in culture, Hannah Arendt argued that the notion of "mass culture" was derived from that of "mass society," which found its place in multiple investigations aiming to shape its intellectual dimension.[1] Things are no longer valued for their nature or the reasons and perspectives of their composition. Rather, they are considered not *interesting* but *acceptable*; and *acceptance* here means not *understanding* but *acquiring*: we can purchase a diploma, publish a book, or even convert values for educating and creating new knowledge into a business. When profit is converted into value and measured—either monetarily or as a good that can be exchanged—things are devalued, lose their meaning, and become mundane and non-divine.

In earlier times, education was a necessity. It was considered a way for self-realization, for the formation of the individual, and for achieving human happiness. Later, it was seen as a possibility for a few—the rich, those belonging to the higher layers of society—and also as a determinant factor for success, a guarantee of stability and social well-being. But today, having been converted from a possession of the few into a product of mass consumption, education has lost some of its value and core characteristics that defined it as an ethical way of composing the individual.

Education is an ethical phenomenon. We share the knowledge that we possess out of a desire to see people around us happier, to eliminate poverty, and to open new doors for understanding social difficulties. Our aim in educating people is to open new horizons for new generations who are interested in reading, writing, and thinking. Action depends on the operation of thinking, and thinking, in turn, determines action. The elimination of poverty and violence is possible through education based on ethical perspectives that consider people to be equal and seeks ways to achieve human happiness.

University life serves the spiritual formation of individuals, conserving, developing, and transmitting cultural characteristics, and realizing the cultural mission of forming not "civilized barbarians" or "non-civilized educated persons" but "civilized educated persons."[2]

And research? Does it have a place in the composition of modern society? Can research offer new space for discussing modern social difficulties? Can we use research data to protect human well-being and prevent the development of many diseases, as well as the emergence of epidemics and pandemics? Research is a new chance, a possibility for creating better educational schemes. If we do not create new knowledge, we will not be successful in transmitting and disseminating what we know or in explaining the necessity of possessing knowledge. Education means tolerance, and tolerance is a fruit of the ethical composition of human beings. We should accept the existence of a diverse and complex human society as a necessary condition for our happiness and better self-realization.

Research should form the basis for teaching. Students learn through close contact with facts, observing and interpreting them using methods of analysis and interpretation. Without proper observation and reflection, it is impossible to acquire true knowledge. That is why teaching should use individual, practical approaches and reasoning.[3]

Universities today compete using sophisticated tools for ranking their activity: how many new bachelor or master programs can they offer to potential students? Which joint PhD programs will help graduates find better jobs? How do they discover new appointments for visiting professorships? How do they attract international students? All these questions are considered when organizing and administering modern universities, often forgetting the basic ethical elements that should underpin all these processes.

If we look through the lists of scientific journals dedicated to the questions of universities and ethics, we will see that their number is fewer compared to journals that study specific branches of philosophy or the work and legacy of individual philosophers. During our library research for this book, we discovered that over the last several decades, the works cited for similar editions were largely the same. In the English-speaking world, authors commonly cite John Henry Newman (1996), Bertrand Russell (2010), John Dewey (1916), Michael Oakeshott (2004), Jaroslav Pelikan (1992), Robert Dearden (1968, 1984), Bill Readings (1999), Ronald Barnett (2011, (ed.) 2012, 2013, 2016, 2022, 2024, 2025), Michael A. Peters (2015, 2019, 2020), Peter Roberts (2013, 2016, 2022), Stefan Collini (2012, 2017), Sharon Rider ((ed.) 2020, (ed.) 2021, 2024a, 2024b), James Arvanitakis and David J. Hornsby ((ed.) 2016, 2022), Christopher Newfield (2004, 2008, 2016), William Pinar (2019, 2023), and Paul Gibbs (2017; Gibbs, de Rijke, Peterson (eds.), 2024). In Spanish texts, Miguel de Unamuno (1902, 1970, 1971), José Ortega y Gasset (2007), Santiago Ramón y Cajal (1952), Francisco Giner de los Ríos (2001), Gregorio Marañon (1956), Julián Marías (1968), and Alfonso Borrero Cabal (2008) are frequently cited. In French, Émile Durkheim (1975), Jean-François Lyotard (1984), Claude Allègre (1993), Isabelle Stengers (2013) and Joleen Masschelein and Maarten Simons (2023) are often referenced. In Russian, Lev Vygotsky (1962), Michail Bachtin (1993), and Vladimer Vernadsky (1908/2002; 1911/2002) are common, and in German, Max Scheler (1921), Karl Jaspers (1959), Martin Heidegger (1989, 2002), Jürgen Habermas (1987), Jürgen Mittelstrass (1994), Norbert Ricken (2006, 2024) and Michael Wimmer (2014) are frequently cited. While there are new texts and authors, the basic methodological apparatus is still composed of classical authors and their texts. These are important but, given the time since their composition, need to be complemented with descriptions and analyses of new challenges faced by modern educational systems. The fact that few texts are published on universities does not mean the topic is out of interest or lacks critical elements for our intellectual development; it just means that we cannot realize its importance and discover the links between the ethical composition of our students and colleagues and the foundations for the well-being of modern civic society.

The interest in reflecting on the university mission should come, first and foremost, from academia. How many universities include classes on university life in their curriculum? On university ethics and on students' enrollment in university life? While teaching courses like "Research Methodology," how often do we include topics that cover the role of research in humanitarian crises, like pandemics, wars, and revolutions? Do we teach our students about the harms that describe the problems frequently accompanying clinical research?[4] Do we dedicate special attention to describing the question of values in medical research?[5] Do we discuss research priorities, including the question of financing medical investigations and the priority given to studies of diseases that affect 10 percent of the world population, neglecting the necessities of the remaining 90 percent?[6]

Another important question is: how do we select the sources for our syllabus? Our observation is that we mostly use textbooks created for concrete university courses and less often use the so-called "companions" or "handbooks." In these editions, researchers publish their recent research data, which appear less in university textbooks and are more critical by nature, whereas textbook chapters represent the generalization of the material and are more descriptive than critical. Students should be familiar with the ethical and other difficulties that represent the everyday reality for future medical investigations.

A transdisciplinary approach should be applied not only to research but also to teaching. The study of pandemics, for instance, should be accompanied by reading not only medical[7] but also classical[8] and literary[9] texts. As the well-being of society is not only a medical but a social problem, the question of humanitarian catastrophes should be discussed from a wider perspective, covering fields of philosophy, history, psychology, public health, and other social and biomedical sciences.

Cosmology and the philosophy of nature underwent dramatic changes at the end of the sixteenth and during the seventeenth centuries when the so-called "scientific revolution" took place. Rethinking Aristotelian ideas of the composition of the world, as well as their incorporation into Catholic doctrine, was critically analyzed by scientists and philosophers, starting from Galileo Galilei's and Isaac Newton's works. This led to the transition from geocentrism to heliocentrism, which, despite great controversy, culminated in the acceptance of non-Aristotelian theories.[10] This was the first step in transforming our views not only on the composition of the universe and our role in it but also for understanding the role of scientific achievements in creating and generalizing new knowledge. Religion, philosophy, psychology of interpersonal relations, and basic human rights were converted into values, admitted, and shared by the modern world community. Hopefully, the progress achieved by the scientific revolution will be deepened, culminating in the long-lasting process of eliminating poverty, intolerance, and violations of basic human rights. As noted, scientific revolutions, in contrast to political and social ones, have more potential for change and produce fewer losses, resulting in a more honorable end of scientific theories compared to theories in other sciences.[11] Research, together with education and ethics, can open new horizons for mutual respect and understanding. This is likely the future of humankind, bringing each of us the dreamed human happiness.

## Notes

1. Arendt, 2006.
2. Pacheco Gómez, 1995, p. 54.
3. Houssay, 1939, pp. 17–18.
4. Stegenga, 2017.
5. Borgerson, 2017.
6. Stegenga, 2018.
7. See Preface, note 3.
8. Such as *On Airs, Waters, and Places* by Hippocrates or Thucydides' description of the great plague at Athens.
9. Such as *A Journal of the Plague Year* by Daniel Defoe, *The Betrothed*, by Alessandro Manzoni, *The Mask of the Red Death* by Edgar Allan Poe, *Death in Venice* by Thomas Mann, *The Abyss* by Margarite Yourcenar, and *The Plague* by Albert Camus.
10. Ladyman, 2002.
11. Mittelstrass, 2018, p. 25.

## Bibliography

Allègre, C. (1993), *L'âge des savoirs: pour une renaiisance de l'Université*, Paris: Gallimard.

Arendt, H. (2006), *Between past and future: eight exercises in political thought*, London: Penguin Books.

Arvanitakis, J. and Hornsby, D. J. (eds.) (2016), *Universities, citizen scholars, and the future of higher education*, London: Palgrave MacMillan Publishers.

Arvanitakis, J. and Hornsby D. J. (2022), "Trust, critical hope and the contemporary university," in Soren S. E. Bengsten and Ryan Gildersleeve (eds.), *Transformation of the university: hopeful futures for higher education*, London: Routledge.

Bakhtin, M. M. (1993), *Toward a philosophy of the act*, Austin: University of Texas Press.

Barnett, R. (2011), *Being a university*, London: Routledge.

Barnett, R. (ed.) (2012), *The future university: ideas and possibilities*, New York: Routledge.

Barnett, R. (2013), *Imagining the university*, London: Routledge.

Barnett, R. (2016), *Understanding the university: Institution, idea, possibilities*, London: Routledge.

Barnett, R. (2022), *The philosophy of higher education: A critical introduction*, London and New York: Routledge.

Barnett, R. (2024), "Scholarship in the university: An ecological perspective," in P. Gibbs, V. de Rijke, A. Peterson (eds.), *The contemporary scholar in higher education*, Cham: Palgrave Macmillan.

Barnett, R. (2025), *Realizing the ecological university. Eight ecosystems, their antagonisms and a manifesto*, London: Bloomsbury.

Borgerson, K. (2017), "Values in medical research," in Miriam Solomon, Jeremy R. Simon, and Havold Kincaid (eds.), *The Routledge companion to philosophy of medicine*, New York and London: Routledge, pp. 319–329.

Borrero Cabal, A. (2008), *La Universidad. Estudio sobre sus orígenes, dinámicas y tendencias*, Bogota: Editorial Pontífica Universidad Javeriana.

Collini, S. (2012), *What Are Universities for?*, London: Penguin.

Collini, S. (2017), *Speaking of universities*, London and New York: Verso.

Dewey, J. (1916), *Democracy and education. The middle works 1899–1924*, vol. 9, Carbondale: Southern Illinois University Press.

Dearden, R. F. (1968), "Happiness and education," *Journal of the Philosophy of Education*, 2 (1), pp. 17–29.

Dearden R. F. (1984), *Theory and practice in education*, London: Routledge and Kegan Paul.

Durkheim, É. (1975), *Educación y sociología*, Barcelona: Península.

Gibbs, P. (2017), *Why universities should seek happiness and contentment?*, London: Bloomsbury.

Gibbs, P., de Rijke, V., Peterson, A. (eds.) (2024), *The contemporary scholar in higher education. Forms, ethos and world view*, Cham: Palgrave Macmillan.

Giner de los Ríos, F. (2001), *La Universidad Española*, Madrid: Civitas.

Habermas, J. and Blazek, J. R. (1987), "The idea of the university: learning processes," *New German Critique*, 41, Special Issue on the Critiques of the Enlightenment (Spring–Summer, 1987), pp. 3–22.

Heidegger, M. (1989), *La autoafirmación de la universidad alemana. El rectorado, 1933-1934: Entrevista a Spiegel*, Madrid: Tecnos.

Heidegger, M. (2002), "Heidegger on the art of teaching," in V. Allen and A. D. Axioti (eds. and trans.), *Heidegger, education, and modernity*, Lanham: Rowman and Littlefield, pp. 27–45.

Houssay, B. (1939), "Recuerdos de un professor y consideraciones sobre la investigación," in Marota P., *El Profesor Bernanrdo A. Houssay (Discursos pronunciados con motivo de su designación como profesor honorario)*, Buenos Aires: Imprenta Universidad de Buenos Aires, pp. 11–27.

Jaspers, K. (1959), *The idea of the university*, Boston: Beacon Press.

Ladyman, J. (2002), *Understanding philosophy of science*, London and New York: Routledge.

Lyotard, J.-F. (1984), *The postmodern condition: a report on knowledge*, Manchester: Manchester University Press.

Marañon, G. (1956), *Vocación y ética y otros ensayos*, Madrid: Espasa-Calpe.

Marías, J. (1968), *El intelectual y su mundo*, Madrid: Espasa-Calpe.

Masschelein, J., Simons, M. (2023), "Remettre « l'école » au coeur de nos établissements d'enseignement. Se réapproprier l'école comme forme pédagogique," *Éthique en éducation et en formation*, 14, pp. 96–112.

Mittelstrass, J. (1994), *Die unzeitgemässe Universität*, Frankfurt am Main: Suhrkamp.

Mittelstrass, J. (2018), *Theoria: chapters in the philosophy of science*, Berlin: De Gruyter.

Newfield, C. (2004), *Ivy and industry: business and the making of the American university, 1880-1980*, Durham, NC: Duke University Press.

Newfield, C. (2008), *Unmaking the public university: The forty-year assault on the middle class*, Cambridge, MA: Harvard University Press.

Newfield C. (2016), *The great mistake: how we wrecked public universities and how we can fix them*, Baltimore, MD: John Hopkins Univ. Press.

Newman, J. H. (1996), *The idea of a university*, New Haven, CT: Yale University Press.

Oakeshott, M. (2004), "The idea of a university," *Academic Questions*, pp. 23–30.

Ortega y Gasset, J. (2007), *Misión de la Universidad*, Madrid: Biblioteca Nueva.

Pacheco Gómez, M. (1995), "Misión de la Universidad," *Anales de la Universidad de Chile*, 2, pp. 51–64.

Pelikan, J. (1992), *The idea of the university: A reexamination*, New Haven: Yale University Press.

Peters, M. A. (2015), *Education, globalization and the state in the age of terrorism*, New York: Routledge.

Peters, M. A. (2019), *The Chinese dream: educating the future: an educational philosophy and theory, Chinese educational philosophy reader, Volume VII*, London: Routledge.

Peters, M. A. (2020), *Wittgenstein, anti-foundationalism, technoscience and philosophy of education: An educational philosophy and theory reader, Volume VIII*, London: Routledge.

Pinar, W. (2019), *What is curriculum theory?* (3rd edition). New York: Routledge.

Pinar, W. (2023), *A praxis of presence in curriculum theory: Advancing currere against cultural crises in education*, London: Routledge.

Ramón y Cajal, S. (1952), *Los tónicos de la voluntad: Reglas y consejos sobre investigación científica*, Buenos Aires: Espasa-Calpe.

Readings, B. (1999), *The university in ruins*, Cambridge, MA: Harvard University Press.

Ricken, N. (2006), *Die Ordnung der Bildung. Beiträge zu einer Genealogie der Bildung*, Wiesbaden: VS Verlag für Sozialwissenschaften.

Ricken, N. (2024), "Über die Zukunft der ›Bildung‹," *Journal für politische Bildung*, 14, 1, pp. 12–16.

Rider, S. (2024a), "Thinking plurality: academic leadership, precarious institutions and collegial bodies as member states in an epistemic union," in Tanya Fitzgerald, Helen M. Gunter and Jon Nixon (eds.), *Intellectual leadership, higher education and precarious times*, London: Bloomsbury Academic.

Rider, S. (2024b), "The contemporary research university: freedom and force," *Social Epistemology review and Reply Collective*, 13 (3), pp. 6–12.

Rider, S., Peters, M. A., Hyvönen, M., Besley, T. (eds.) (2020), *World class universities. Evaluating education: normative systems and institutional practices*, Singapore: Springer.

Rider, S., Peters, M. A., Hyvönen, M., Besley, T. (eds.) (2021), "The corrosion of academic character," in Áine Mahon (ed.), *The Promise of the University Reclaiming Humanity, Humility, and Hope*, vol. 10, Singapore: Springer.

Roberts, P. (2013), "Happiness, despair and education," *Studies in Philosophy and Education*, 32, pp. 463–475.

Roberts, P. (2016), *Happiness, hope, and despair: rethinking the role of education*, New York: Peter Lang.

Roberts, P. (2022), *Paulo Freire*, New York: Peter Lang.

Russell, B. (2010), *On education*, London and New York: Routledge.

Scheler, M. (1921), "Universität und Volkshochschule," in Leopold von Wiese (Hg.), *Soziologie des Volksbildungswesens*, München/Leipzig: Duncker and Humblot, pp. 153–91.

Stegenga, J. (2017), "Measuring harms," in Miriam Solomon, Jeremy R. Simon, and Harold Kincaid (eds.), *The Routledge companion to philosophy of medicine*, New York and London: Routledge, pp. 342–352.

Stegenga, J. (2018), *Care and cure. An introduction to philosophy of medicine*, Chicago and London: The University of Chicago Press.

Stengers, I. (2013), *Une autre science est possible! Manifeste pour un ralentissement des sciences*, Paris: Éditions La Découverte.

Unamuno, M. de (1902), "Acerca de los exámenes," *El Imparcial*, 13.X.

Unamuno, M. de (1970), *Obras Completas, VIII*, Madrid: Escelicer.

Unamuno, M. de (1971), *Obras Completas, IX*, Madrid: Escelicer.

Vernadsky, V. (1908/2002), "Academic life," in Vladimir Vernadsky, *On science*, 2, Saint Petersburg: Russian Christian Humanitarian Institute, pp. 168–176.

Vernadsky, V. (1911/2002), "Crush," in Vladimir Vernadsky, *On science*, Saint Petersburg: Russian Christian Humanitarian Institute, pp. 177–181.

Vygotski, L. (1962), *Thought and language*, Cambridge, MA: MIT Press.

Wimmer, M. (2014), *Pädagogik als Wissenschaft des Unmöglichen. Bildungsphilosophische Interventionen*, Paderborn: Ferdinand Schöningh Verlag.

# Index

**A**
Aristotle 18, 119

**B**
Bentham, Jeremy 121
*Bildung* 11, 53–54,

**C**
customs 17

**D**
deduction 76
Dewey, John 15, 29, 31, 33–37, 72, 137

**E**
education 9–11, 15, 18–19, 21–23, 29–39, 53–59, 71–75, 85–91
  antiracist 56
  distance 90
  emergency remote 90
  intercultural 56
  multicultural 19, 55–6
  of minorities 56
  ethics 10, 18–19, 30, 55, 123, 137–39
  medical 92

**F**
Fichte, Johann Gottlieb 53–54
Froebel, Friedrich 29–32

**G**
García Berrio, Antonio 122
Georgia 23, 105
Google Scholar 77, 110

**H**
happiness 119
  human 119
health 11, 17, 21
  communication 22
Hegel, Georg Wilhelm 29–30
Herbart, Johann Friedrich 30, 36
Houssay, Bernardo A. 71, 108, 111

Humboldt, Alexander von 53–54
Hume, David 119–120

**I**
induction 76
interdisciplinarity 74

**K**
Kant, Immanuel 85, 112
knowledge 15–16, 19
  biomedical 91
  illness-related 58
  lay 76, 91
  social science 91

**M**
method 10, 15, 22
  axiomatic 76
  hypothetico-deductive 76
  inductive-deductive 76
  mixed method 78, 92
  qualitative 93
  quantitative 93
Mill, James 121
Mill, John Stuart 119
Mittelstrass, Jürgen 11, 137
Montessori, Maria 38

**N**
Natorp, Paul 29, 36
nonsense 11

**O**
Oakeshott, Michael 72, 137
Ortega y Gasset, José 29, 36

**P**
pandemic 10, 21, 78
  COVID- 19, 78, 88, 94, 115
  H5N1 21
París, Carlos 106
peer-review 75, 109, 111, 132
Piaget, Jean 29, 38

INDEX

Pestalozzi, Johann Heinrich 29, 31
Peter Lang 109, 131
Plato 18, 37, 54, 119
public health 11, 17, 22, 71
    mental health 21
    research 9, 15, 71

**R**
Ramón y Cajal, Santiago 108, 137
Readings, Bill 11, 75, 85, 112, 132, 137
Rhetoric 122
    Cultural 122
    of Argumentation 122
    General Textual 122
    Structuralist 122
Rousseau, Jean-Jacques 29, 32, 54
Rustaveli Foundation 110
*ruins* 11
Russell, Bertrand 29, 39, 87, 137

**S**
Schleiermacher, Friedrich 53
Scopus 77, 109
Socrates 17

**T**
transdisciplinarity 74, 78

**U**
Unamuno, Miguel de 29, 33, 137

**V**
values 35, 37,
    ethical 74
    non-universal 20
    universal 20
Vernadsky, Vladimir 73, 87, 137

# OMPLiCATED

## A BOOK SERIES OF CURRICULUM STUDIES

Reframing the curricular challenge educators face after a decade of school deform, the books published in Peter Lang's Complicated Conversation Series testify to the ethical demands of our time, our place, our profession. What does it mean for us to teach now, in an era structured by political polarization, economic destabilization, and the prospect of climate catastrophe? Each of the books in the Complicated Conversation Series provides provocative paths, theoretical and practical, to a very different future. In this resounding series of scholarly and pedagogical interventions into the nightmare that is the present, we hear once again the sound of silence breaking, supporting us to rearticulate our pedagogical convictions in this time of terrorism, reframing curriculum as committed to the complicated conversation that is intercultural communication, self-understanding, and global justice.

The series editor is

> Dr. William F. Pinar
> Department of Curriculum Studies
> 2125 Main Mall
> Faculty of Education
> University of British Columbia
> Vancouver, British Columbia V6T 1Z4
> CANADA

To order other books in this series, please contact our Customer Service Department:

> peterlang@presswarehouse.com (within the U.S.)
> orders@peterlang.com (outside the U.S.)

Or browse online by series:

> www.peterlang.com

www.ingramcontent.com/pod-product-compliance
Lightning Source LLC
Chambersburg PA
CBHW052025290426
44112CB00014B/2380